Anime Coloring Book
Volume 2

Jessica Metzger

Copyright © 2021 Jessica Metzger.

All rights reserved. No part of this work may be reproduced, distributed, or transmitted in any form or by any means, including photocopying, recording, or other electronic or mechanical methods, without the prior written permission of the author, except in the case of brief quotations embodied in critical reviews and certain other noncommercial uses permitted by copyright law.

Art by Jessica Metzger.

Book design by Jessica Metzger.

Published by Metzger Publishing, Fairfax, Virginia, United States of America.

MetzgerPublishing@Gmail.com

First printing edition 2021

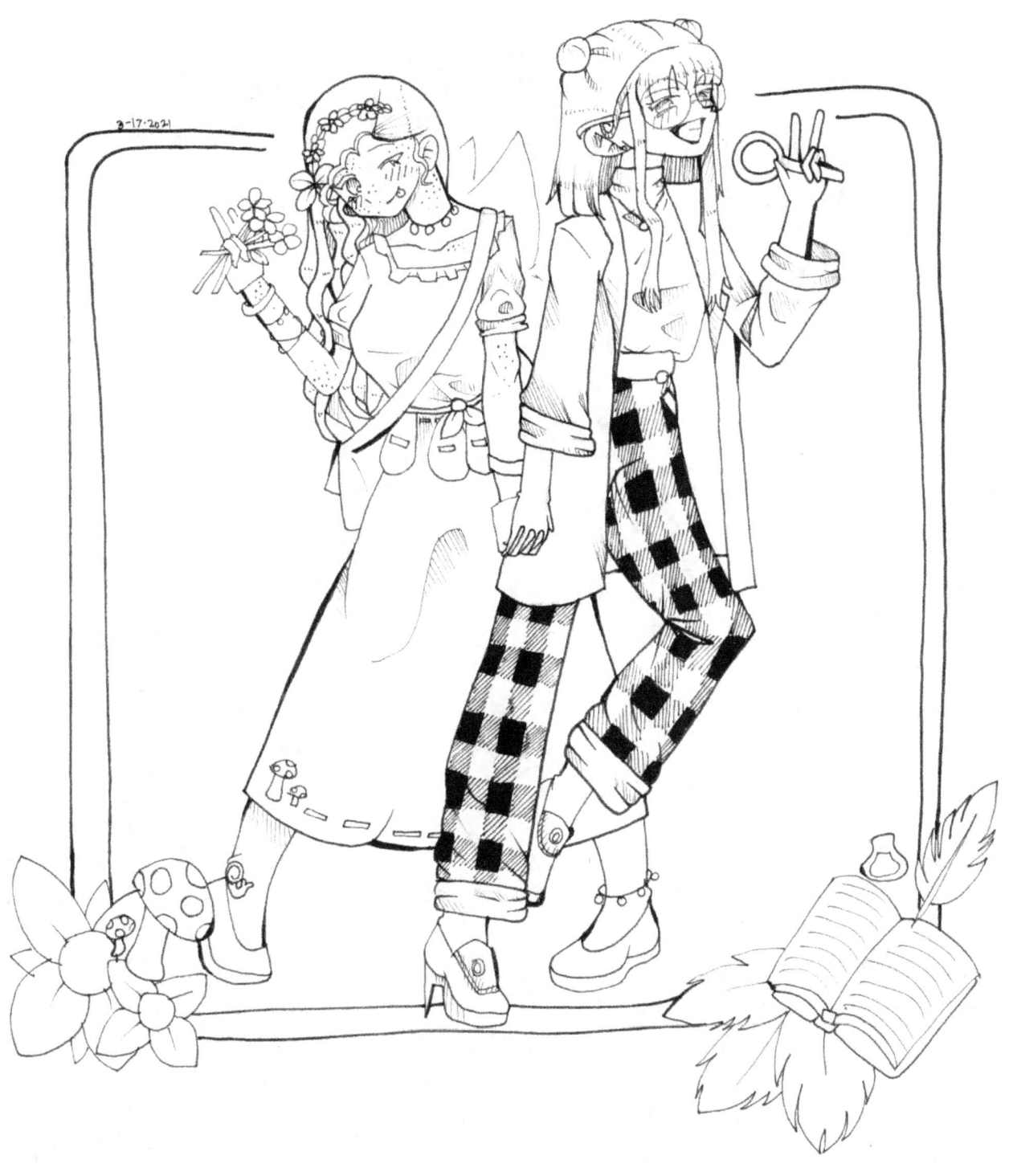

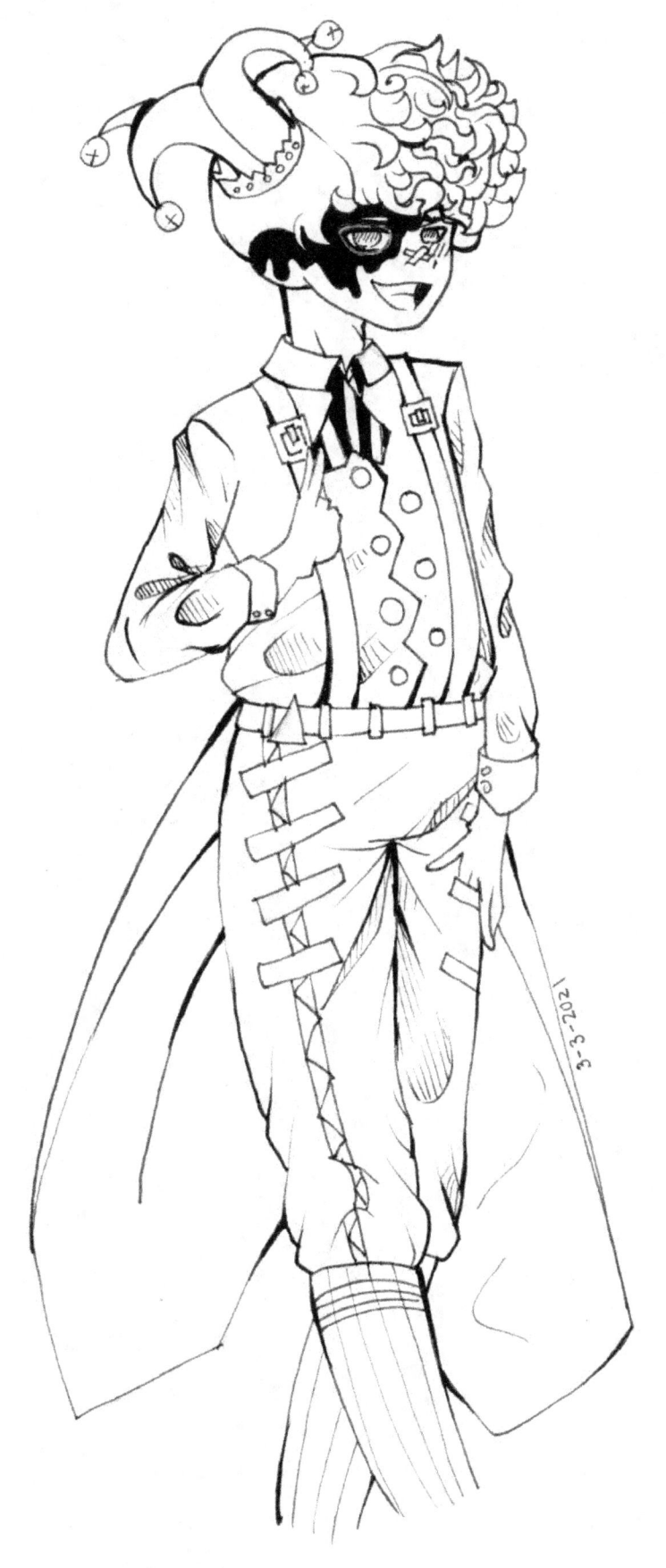

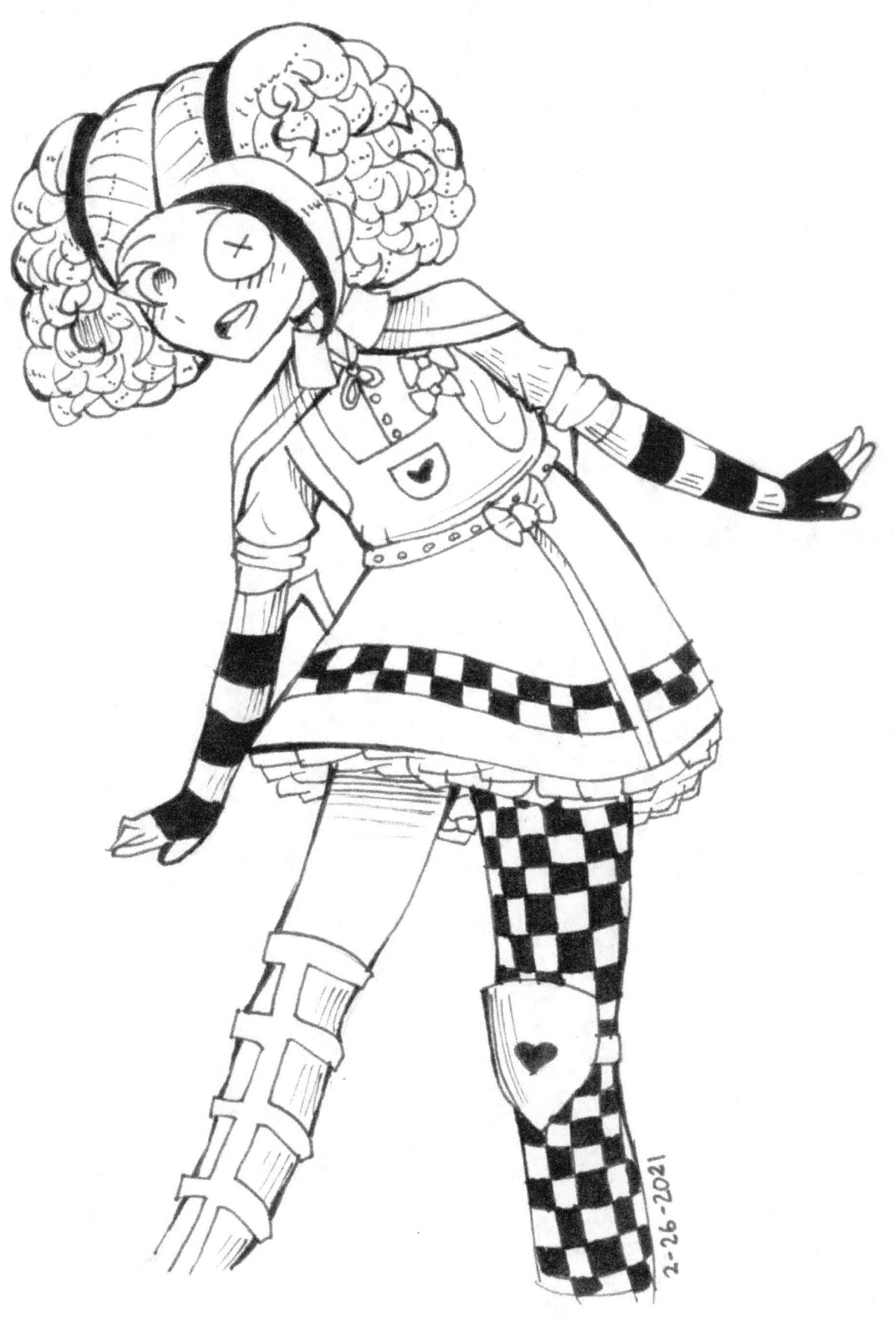

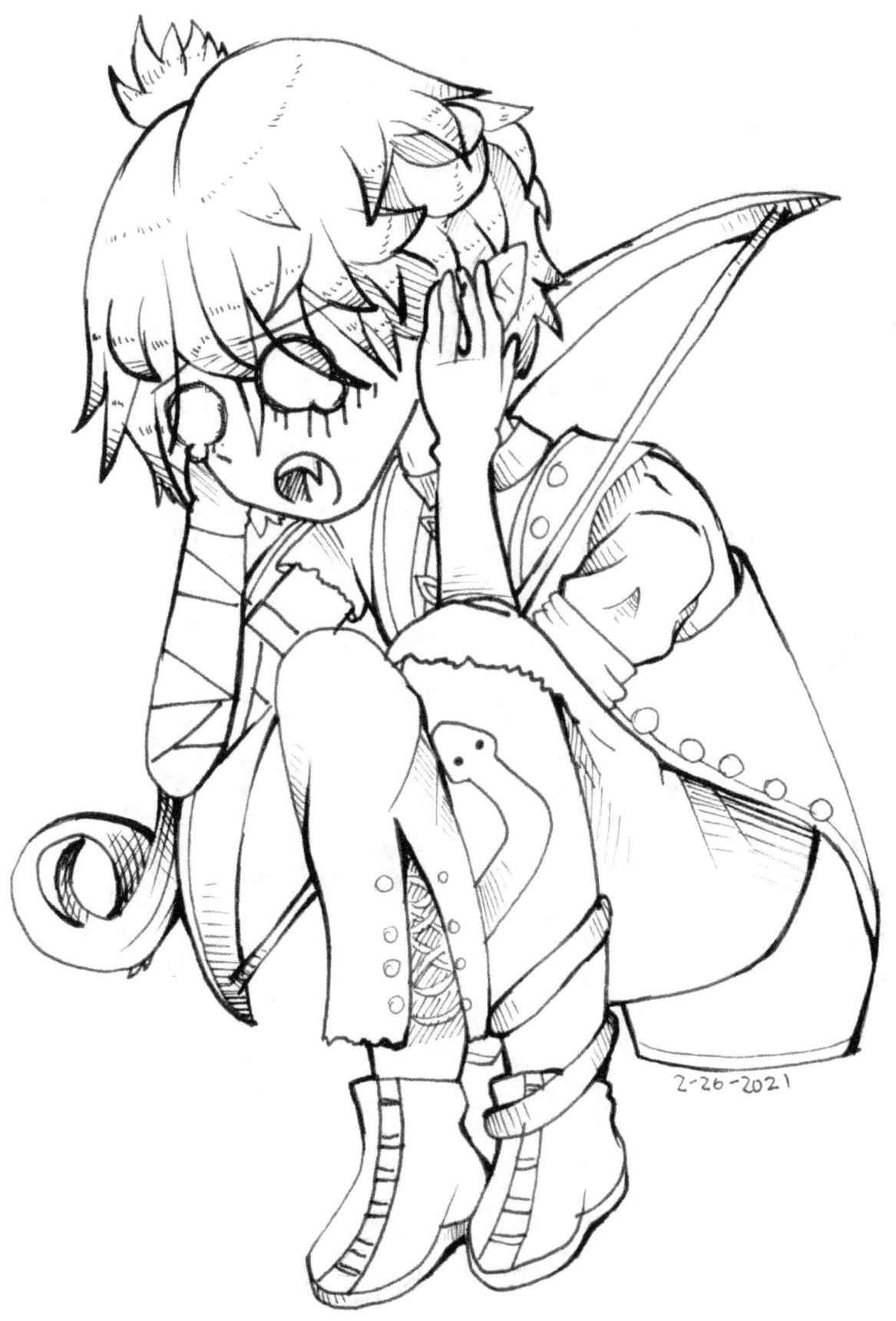

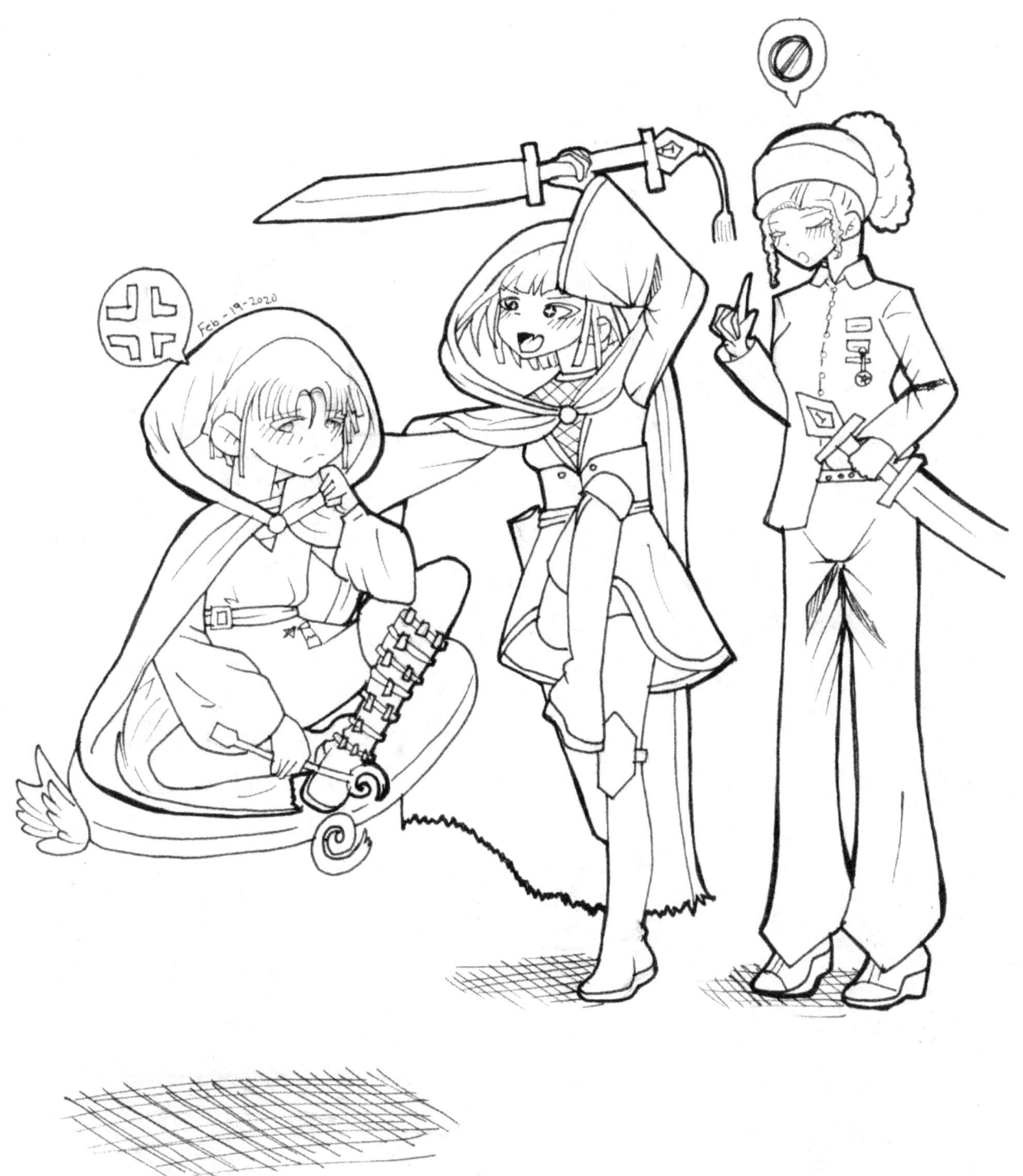

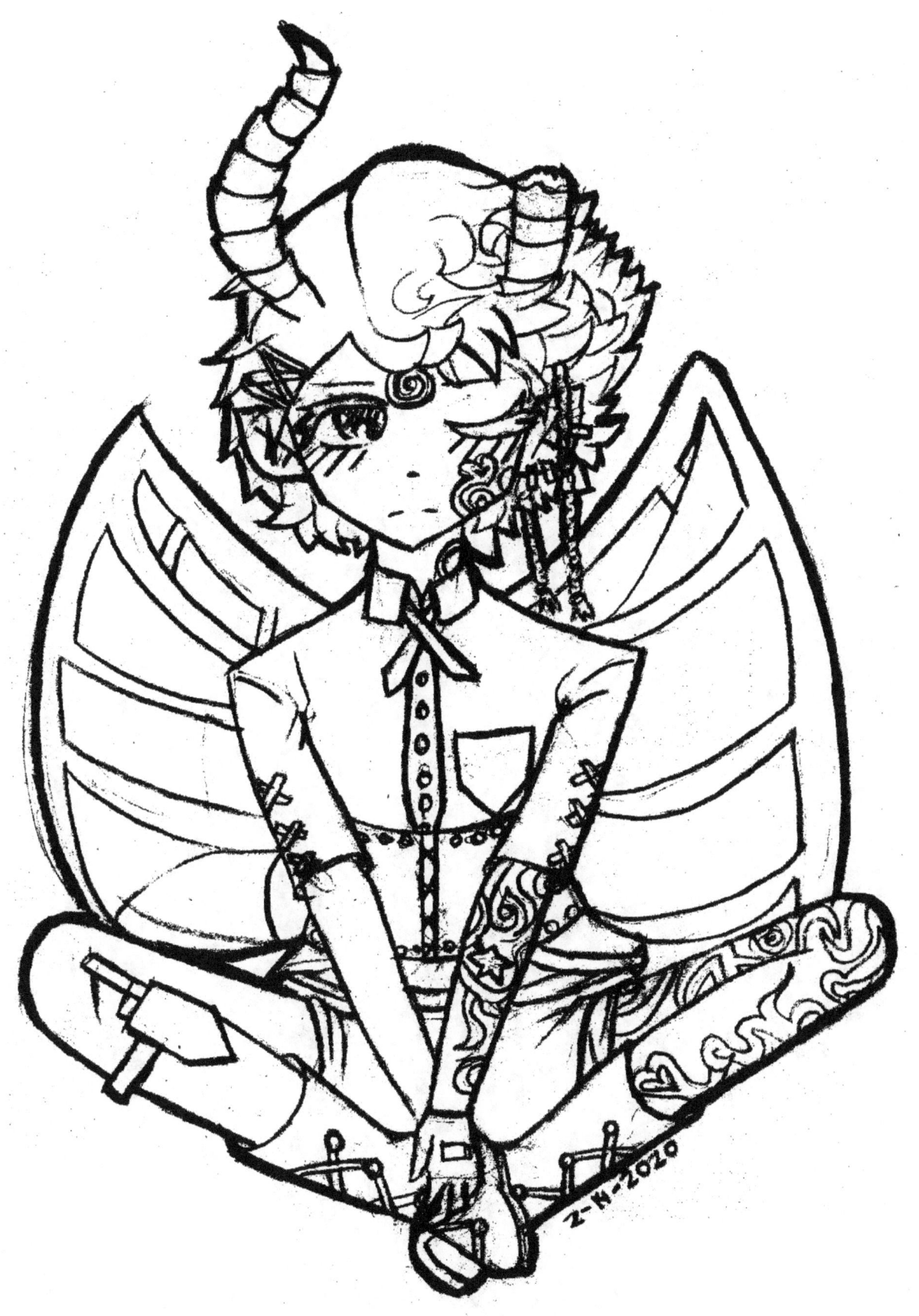

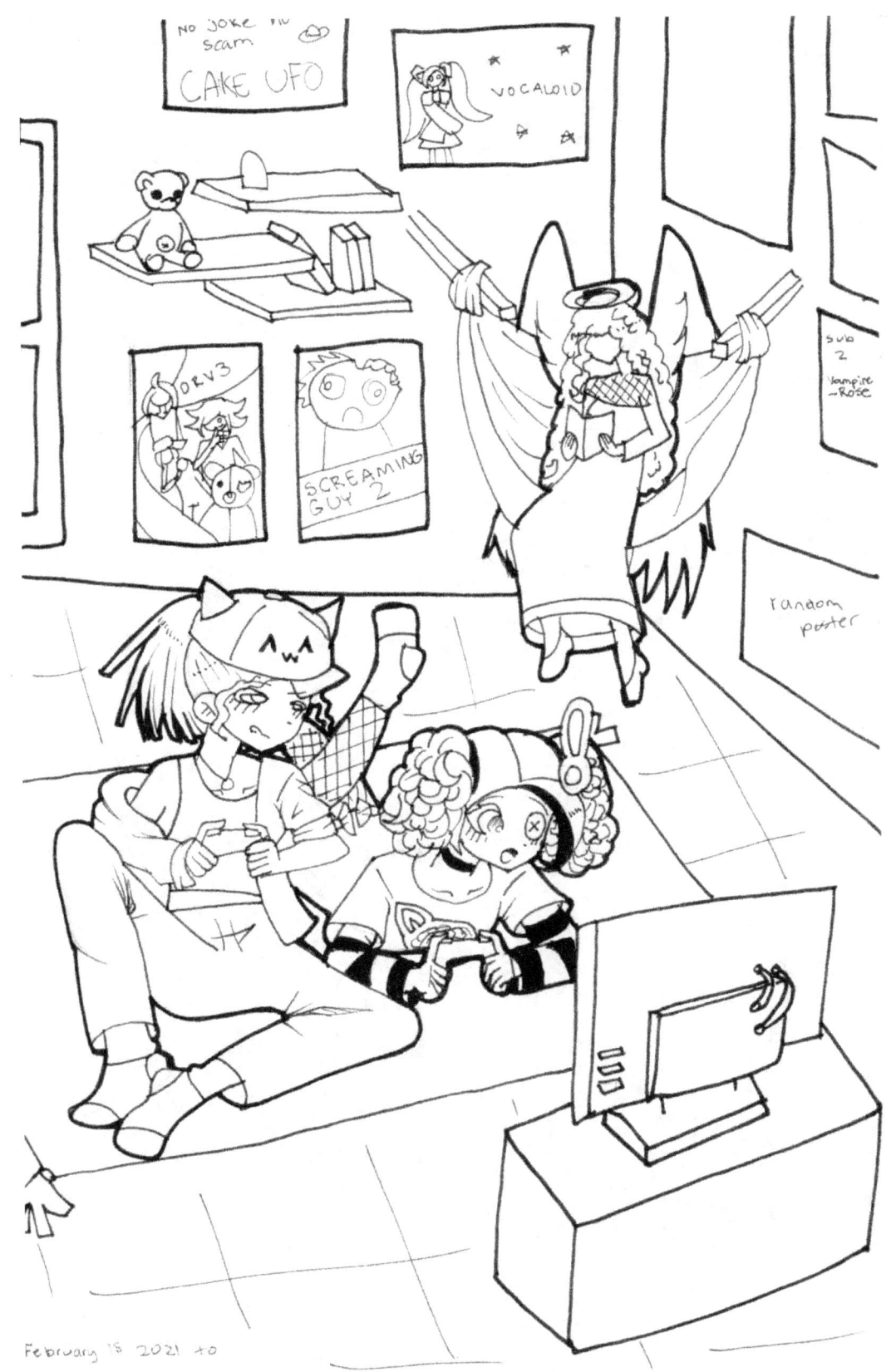

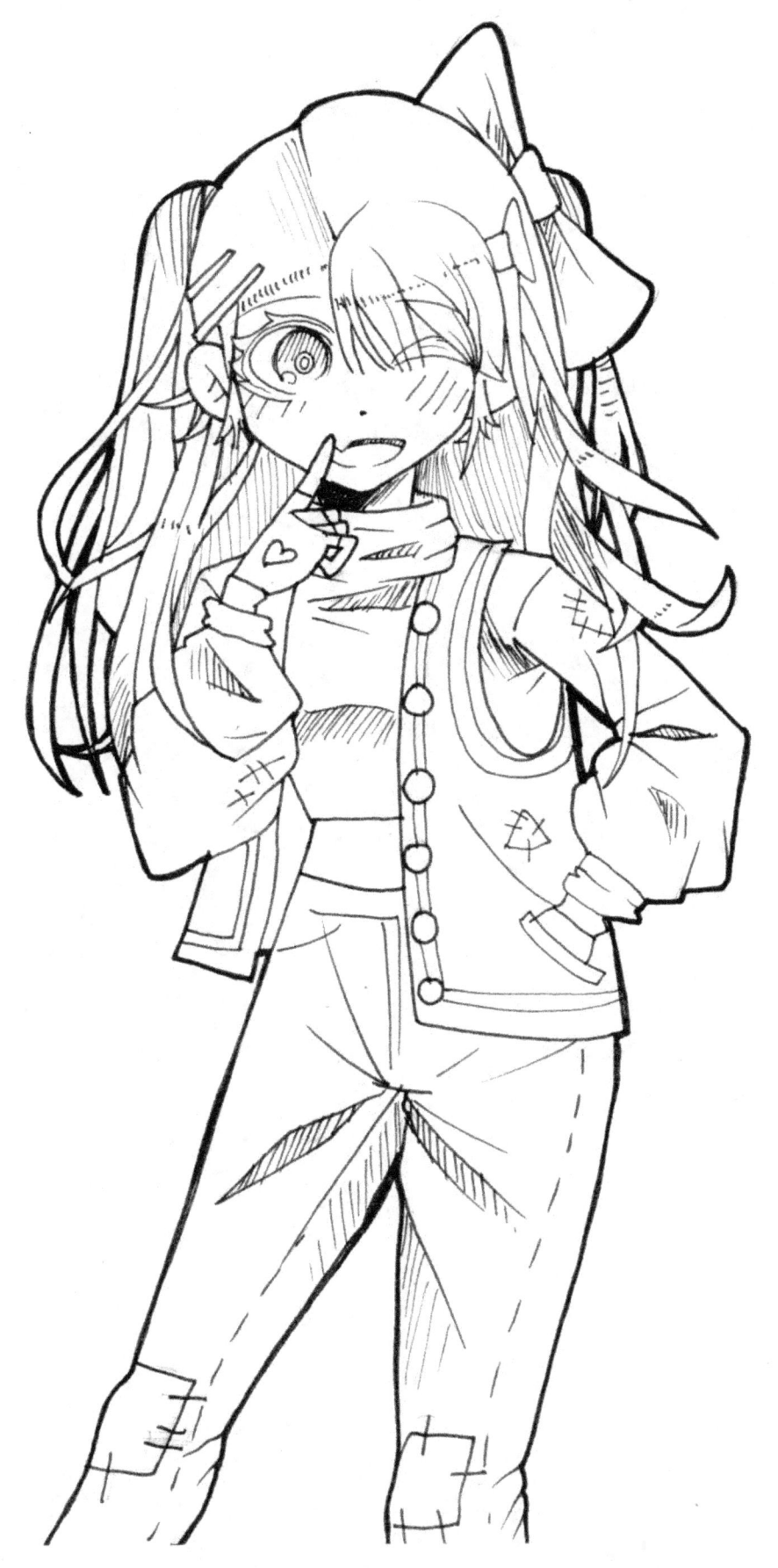

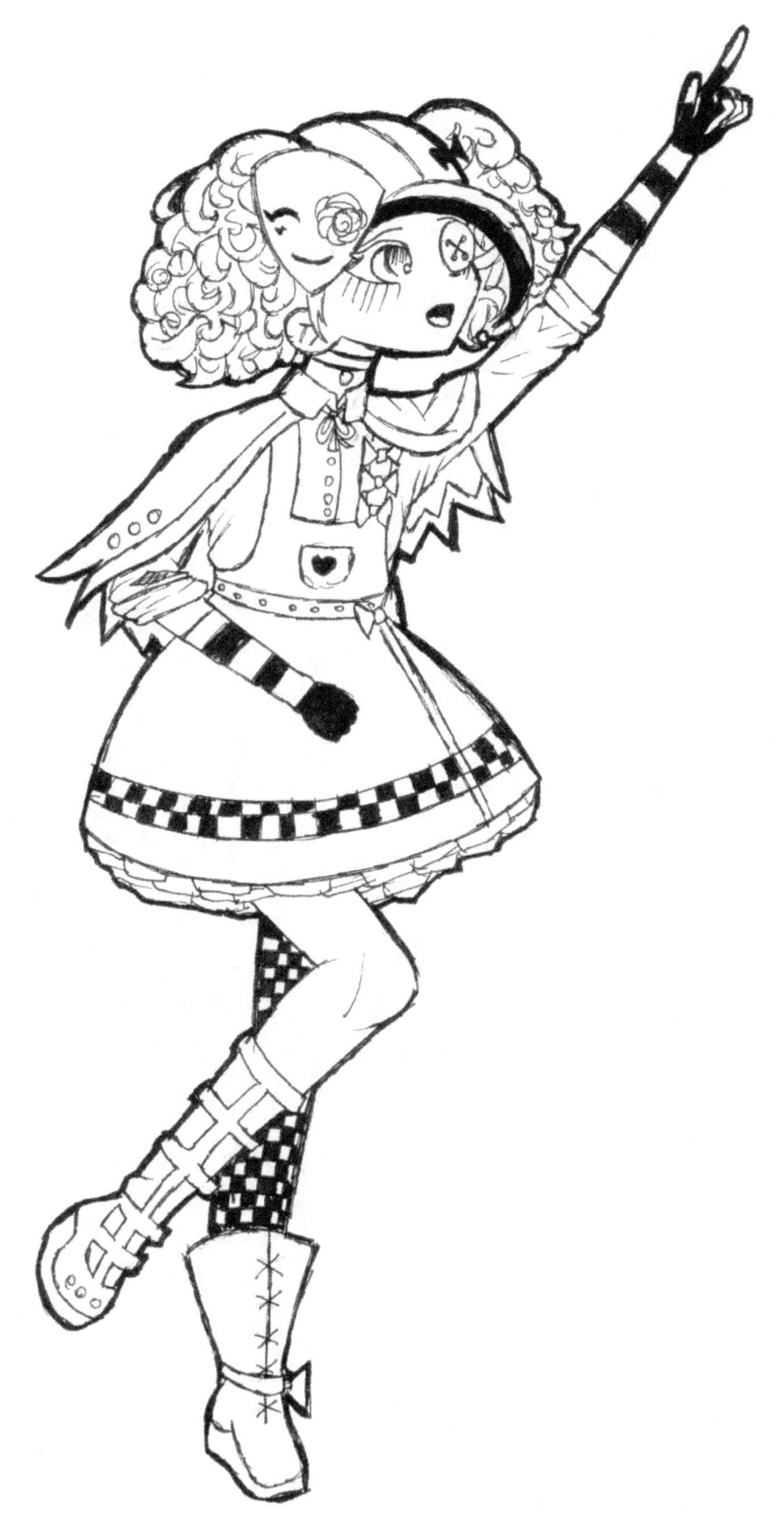

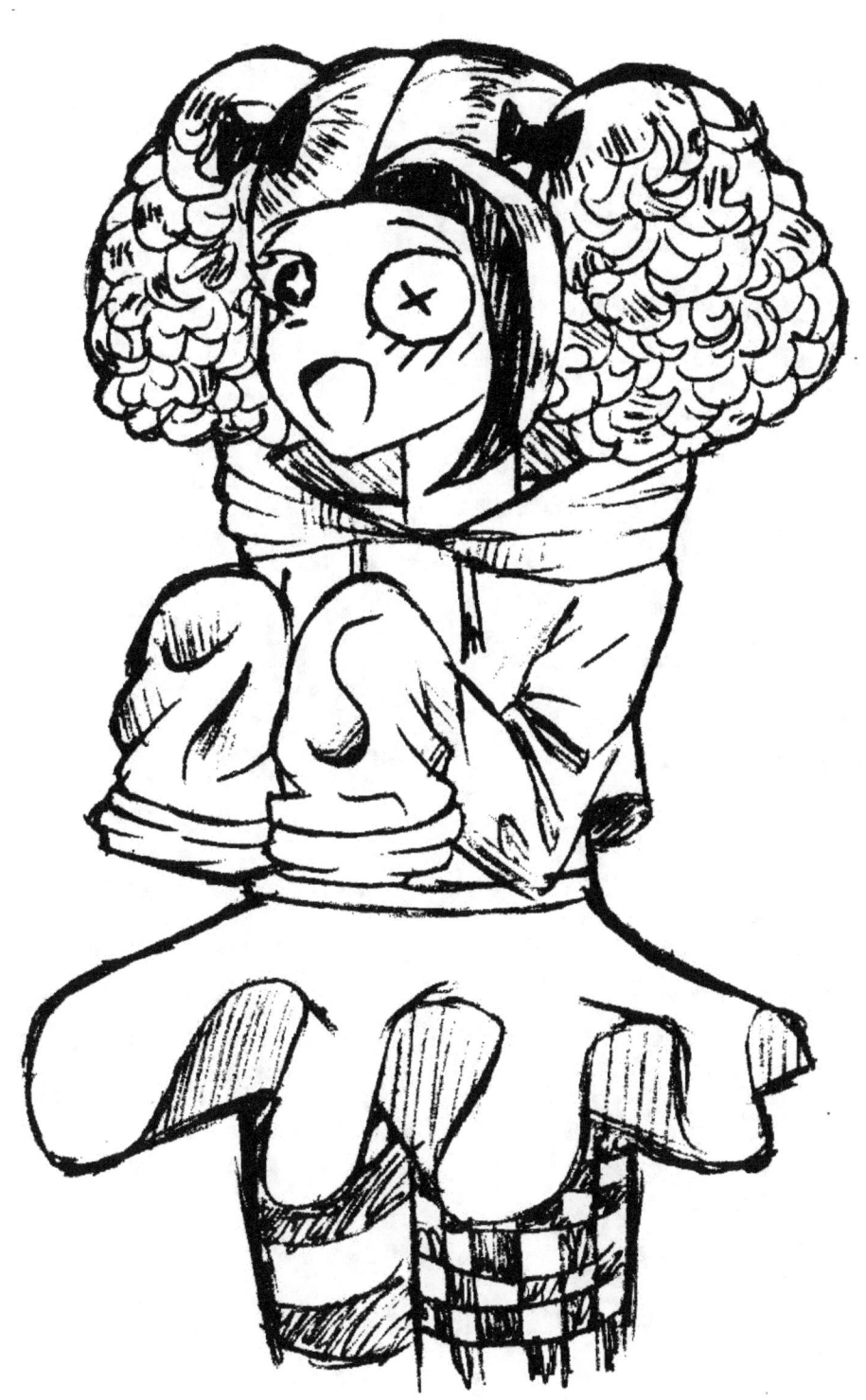

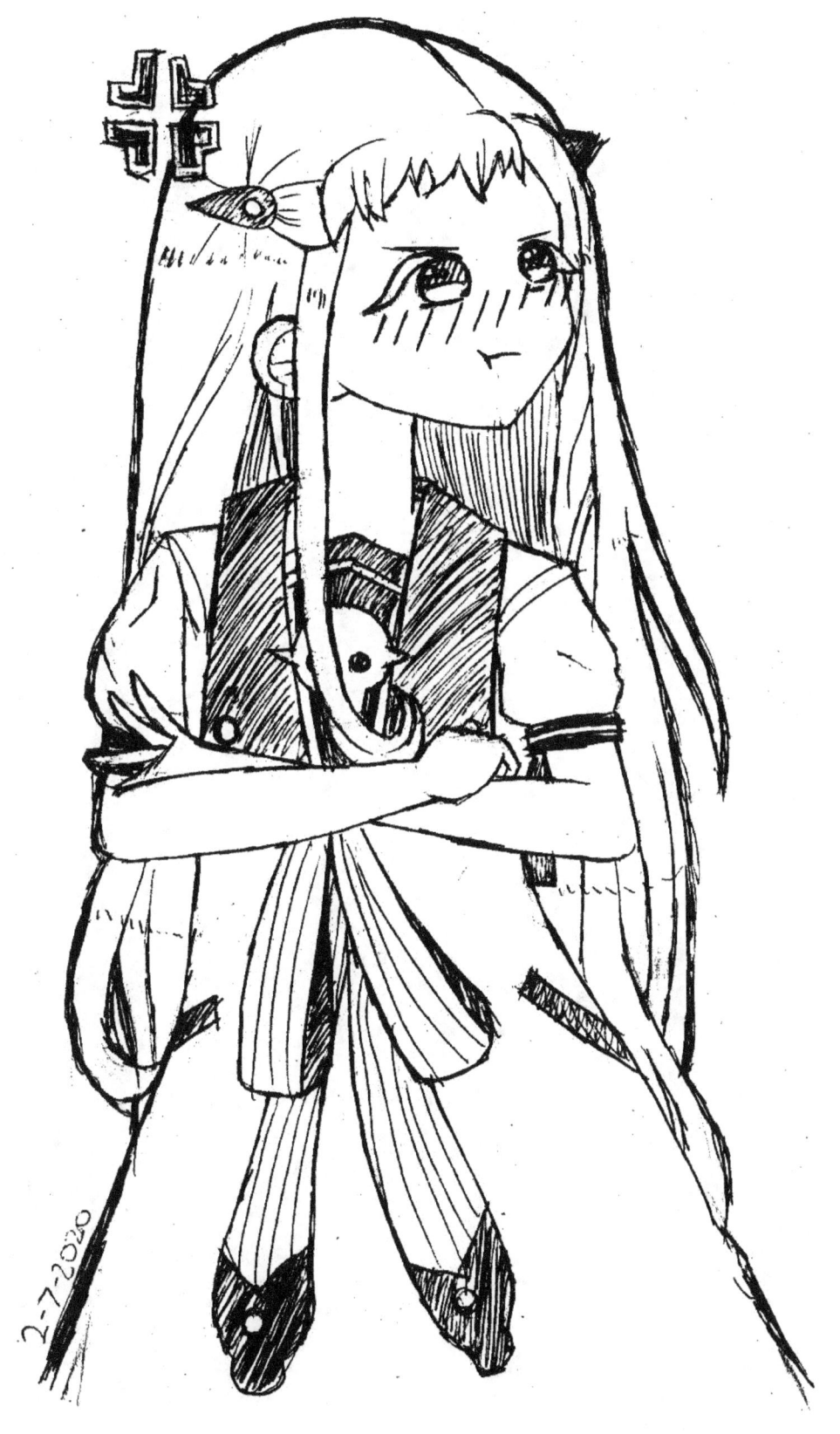

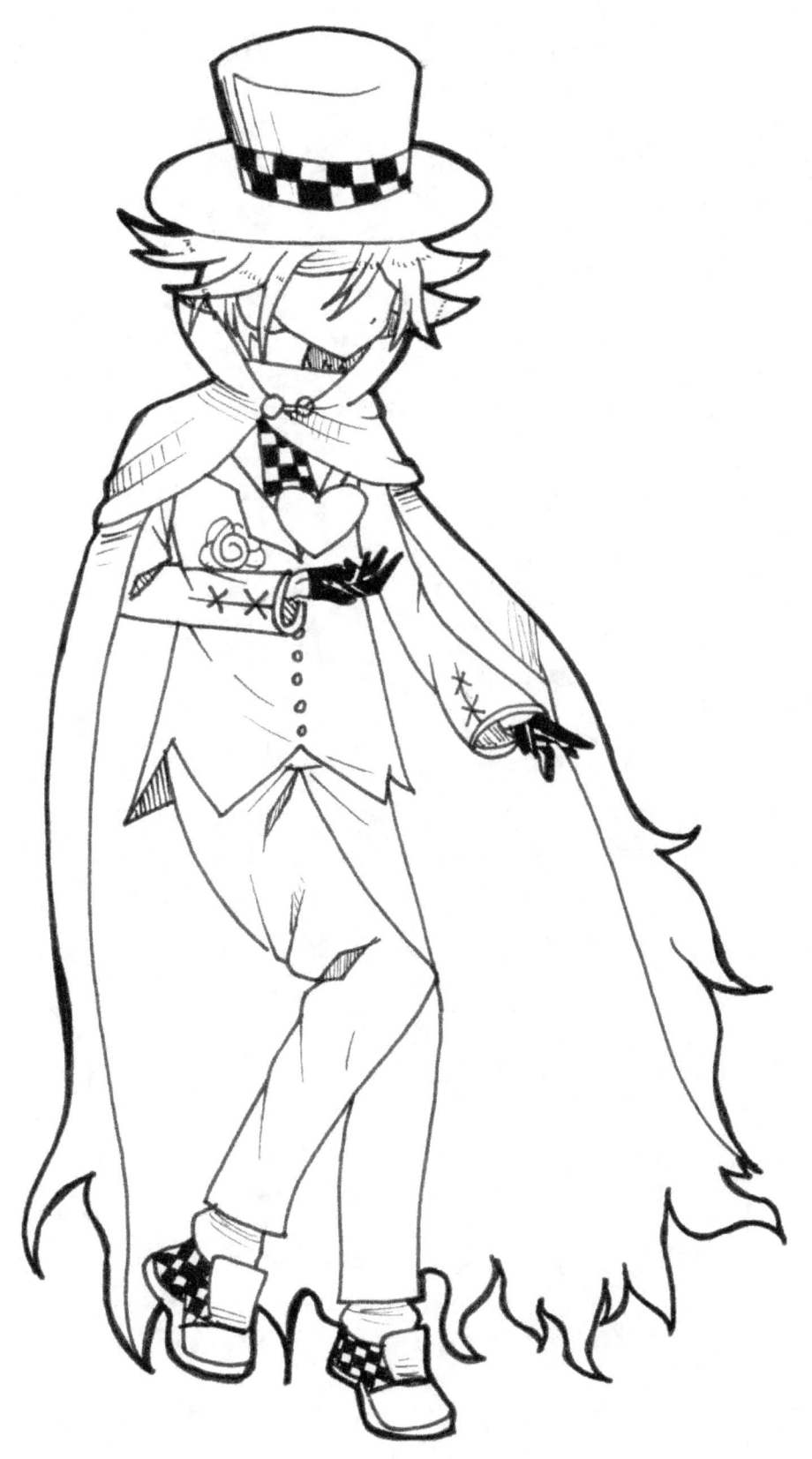

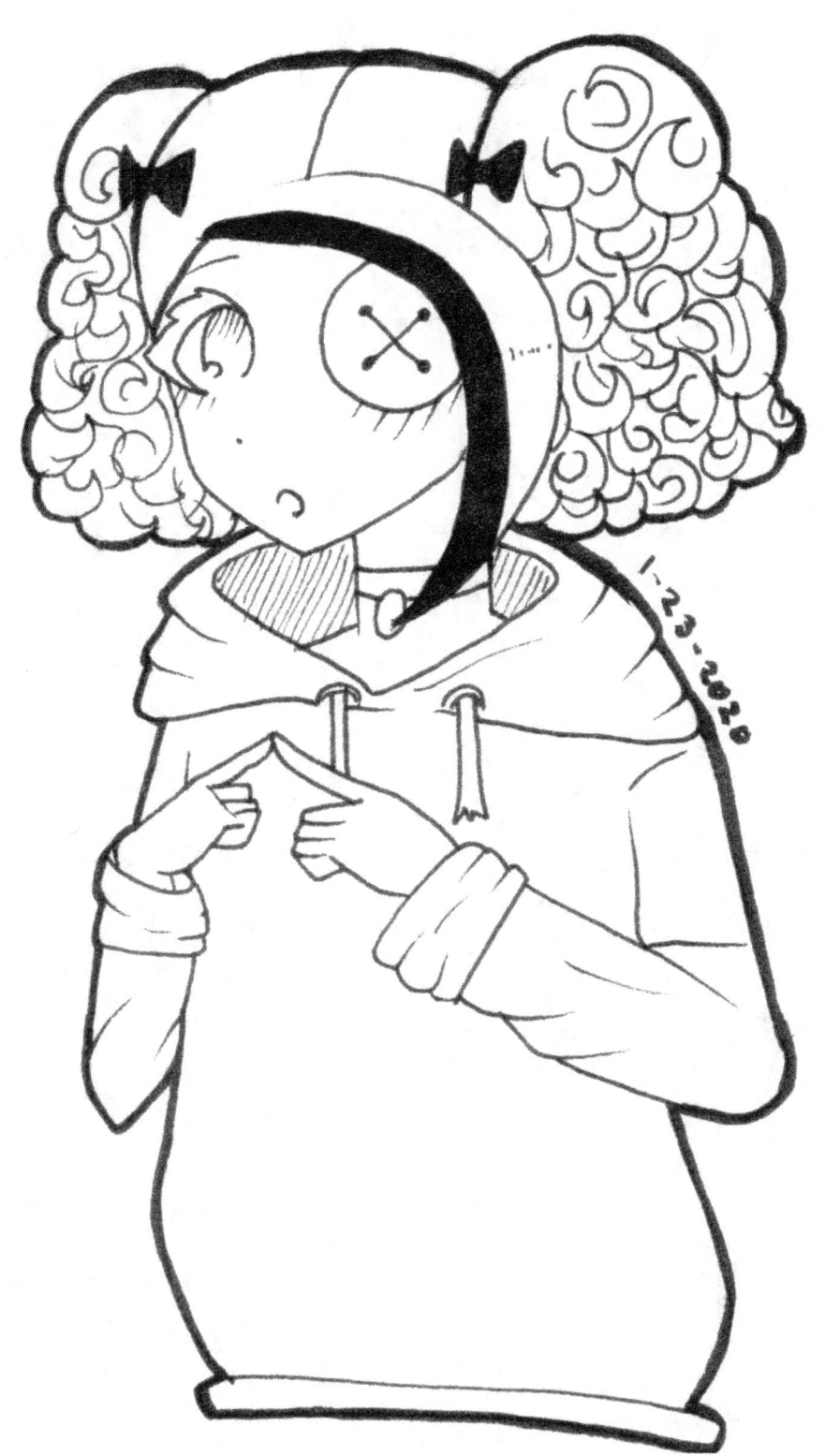

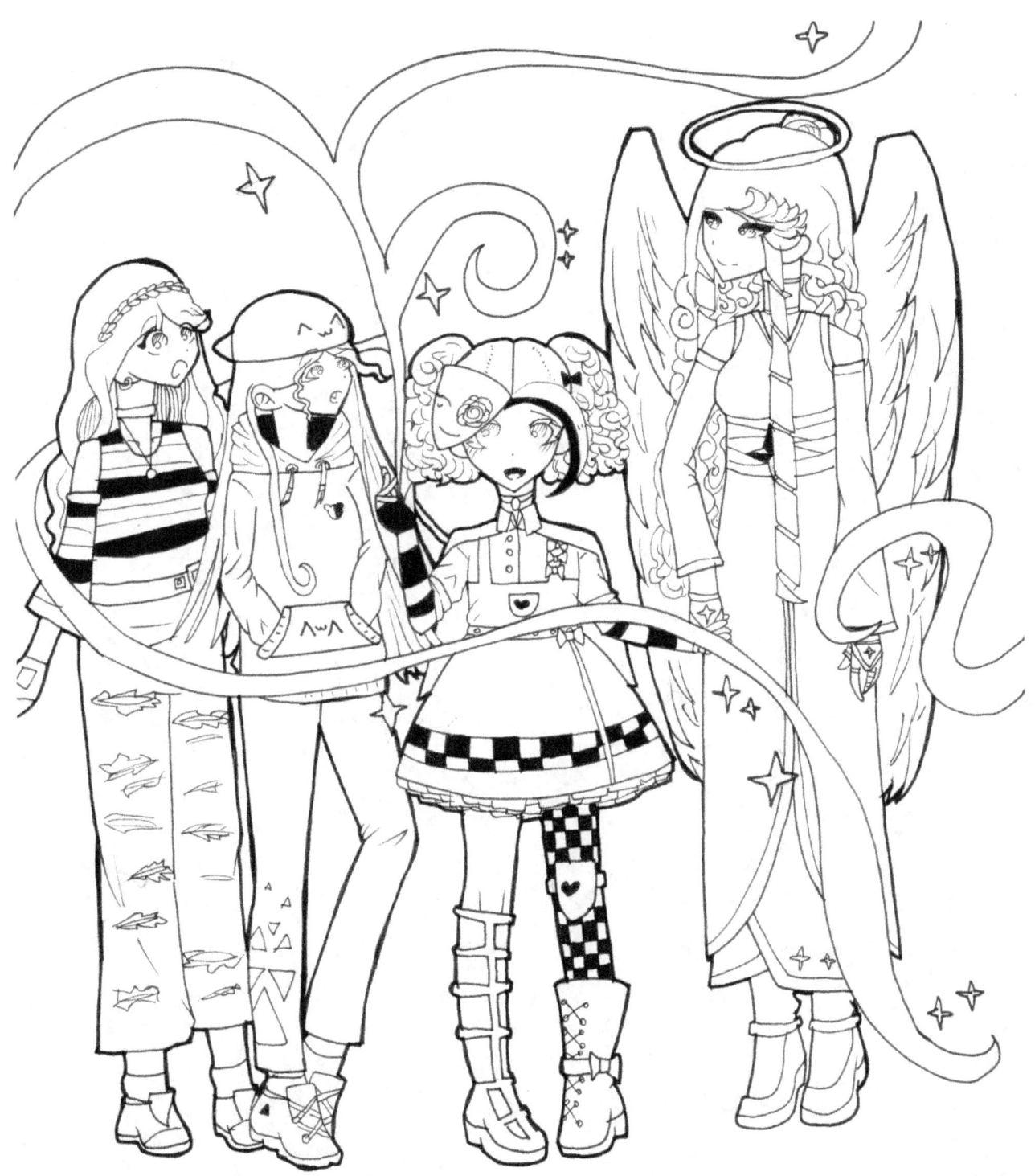

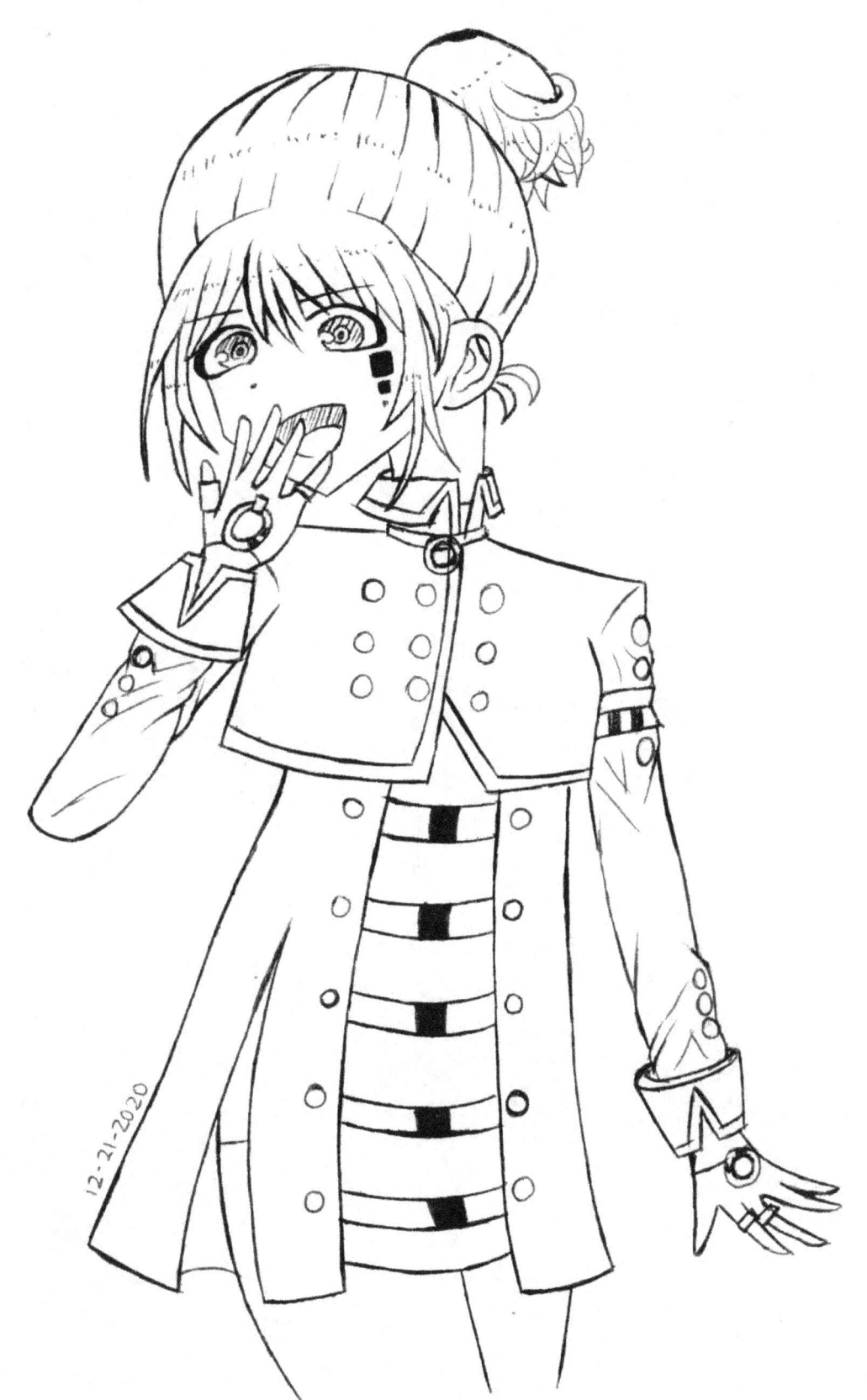

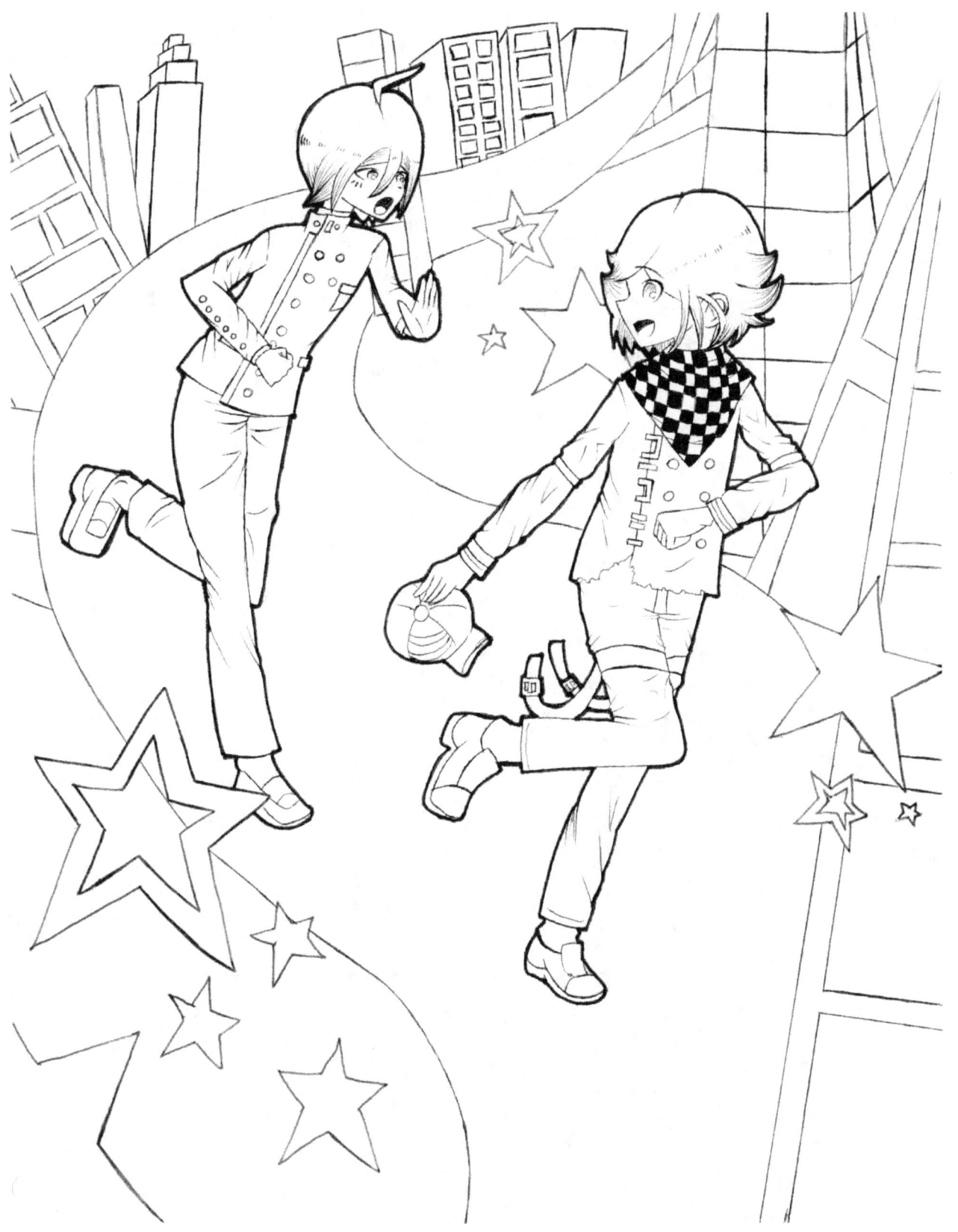

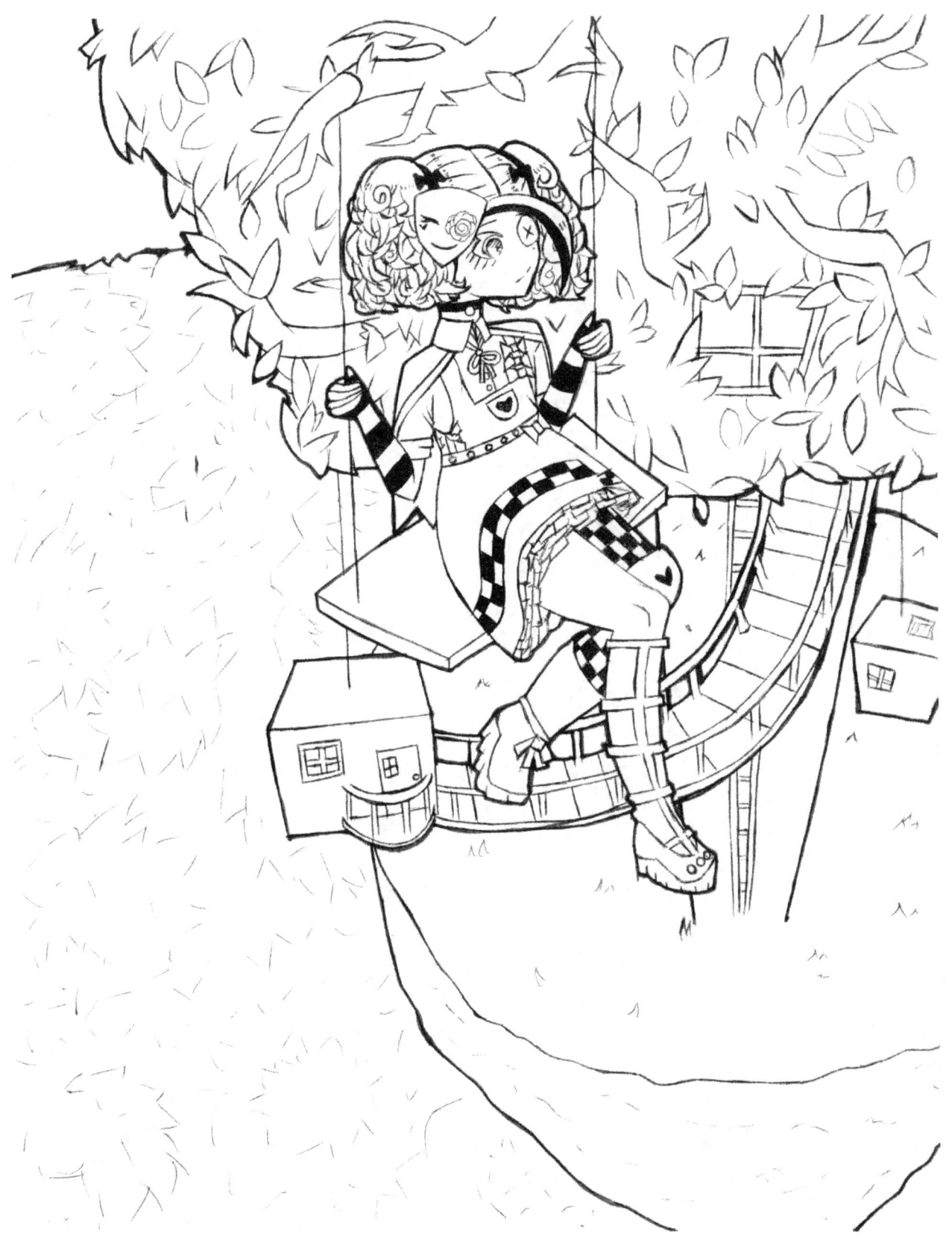

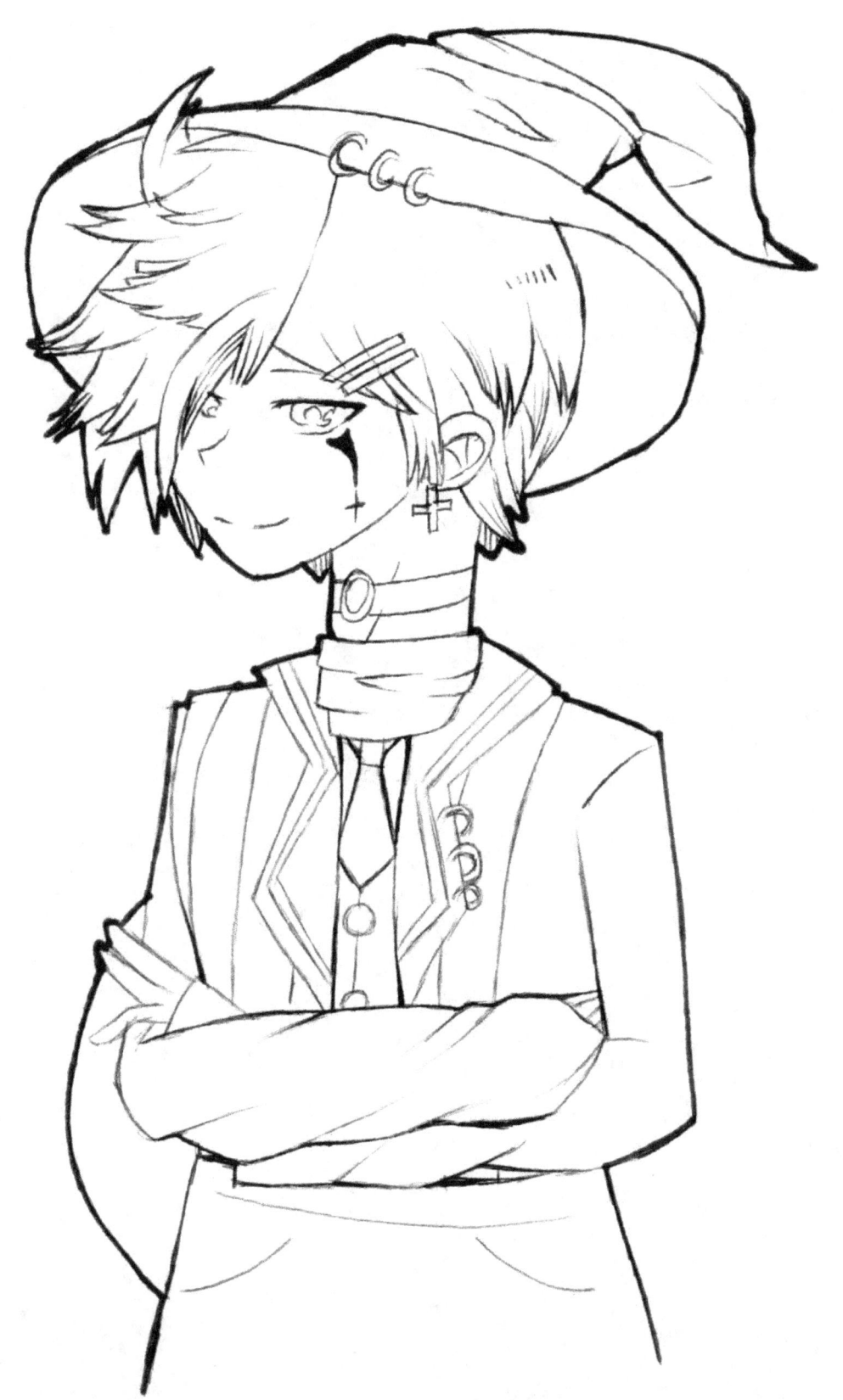

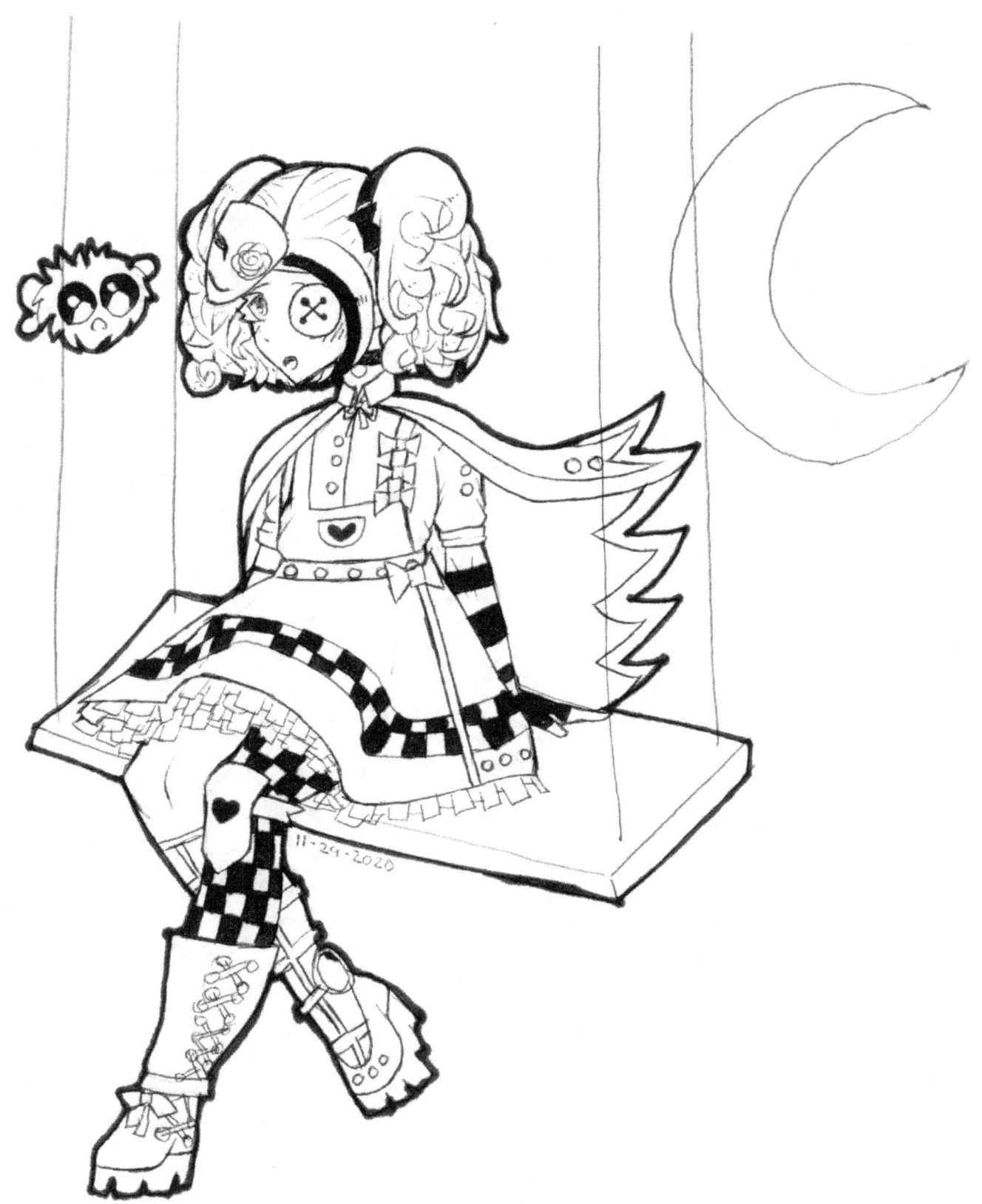

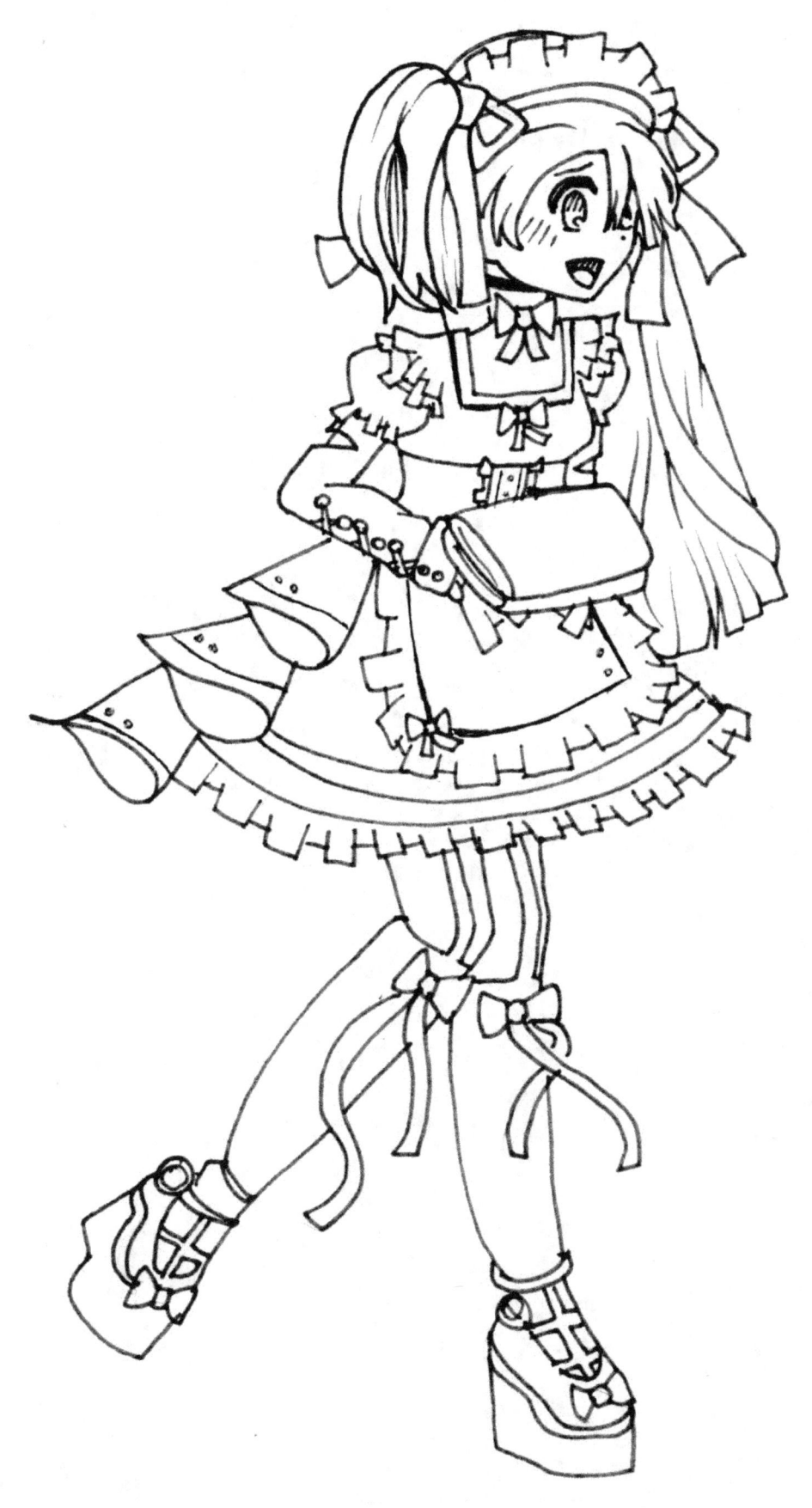

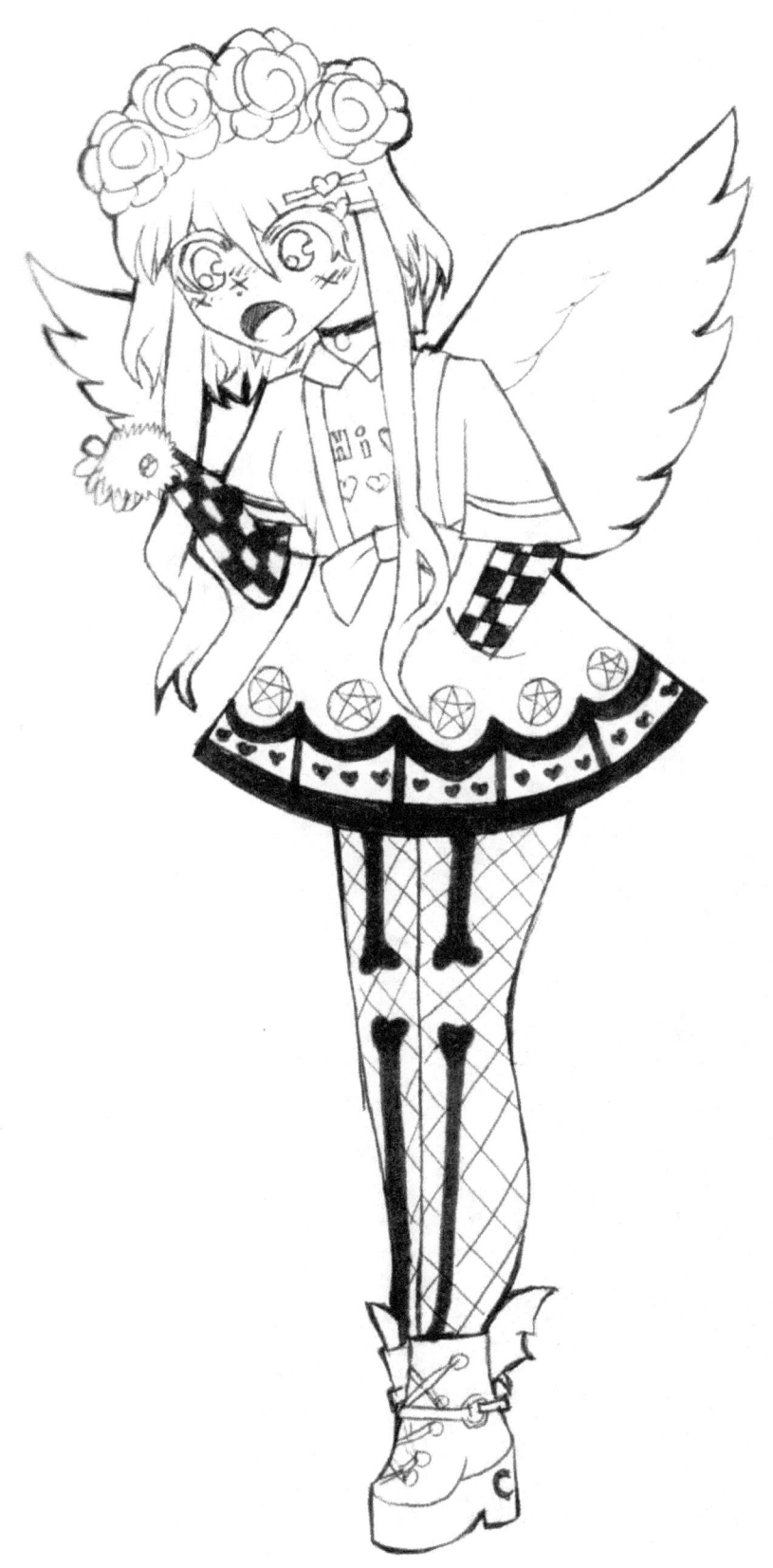

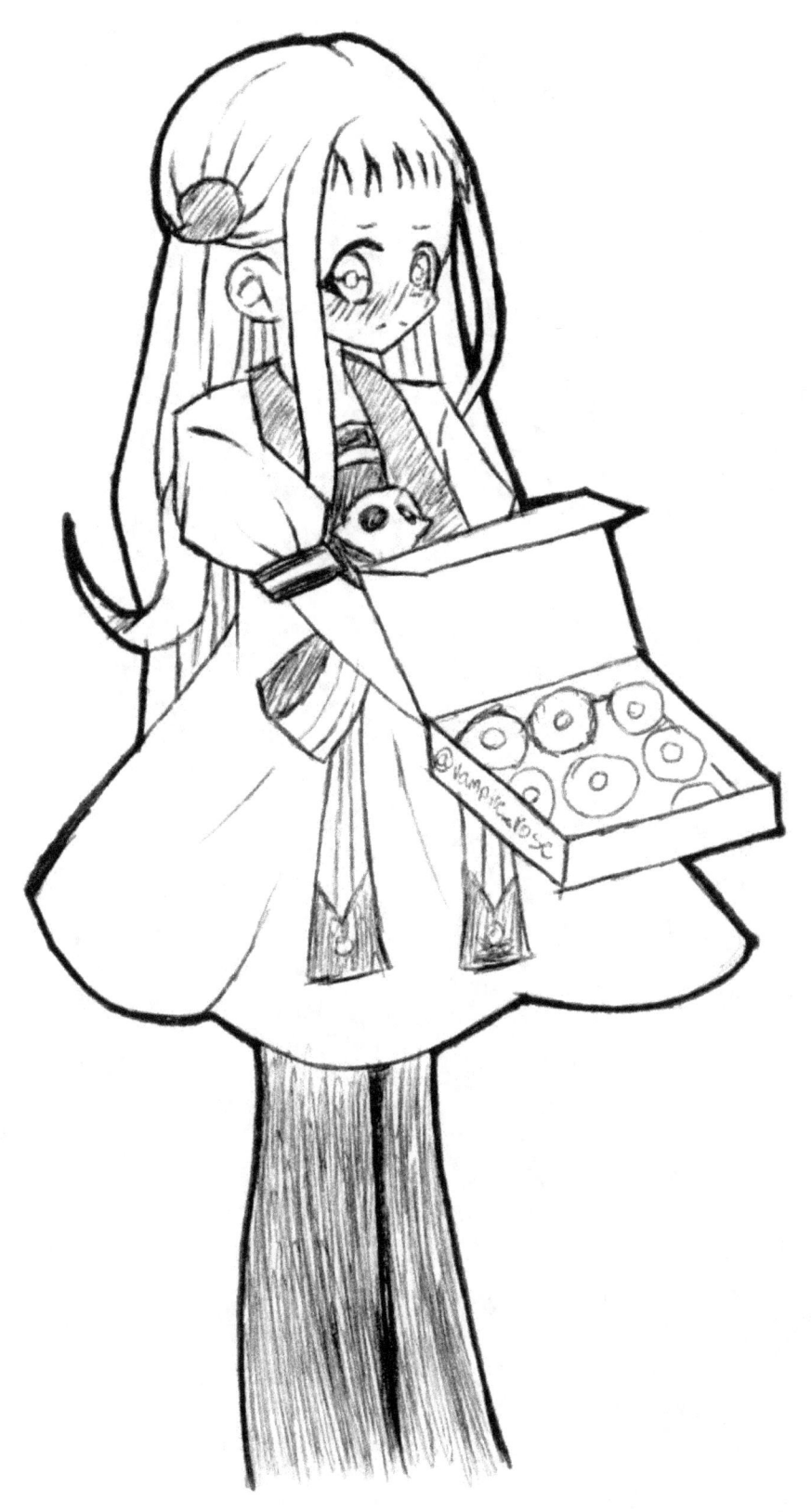

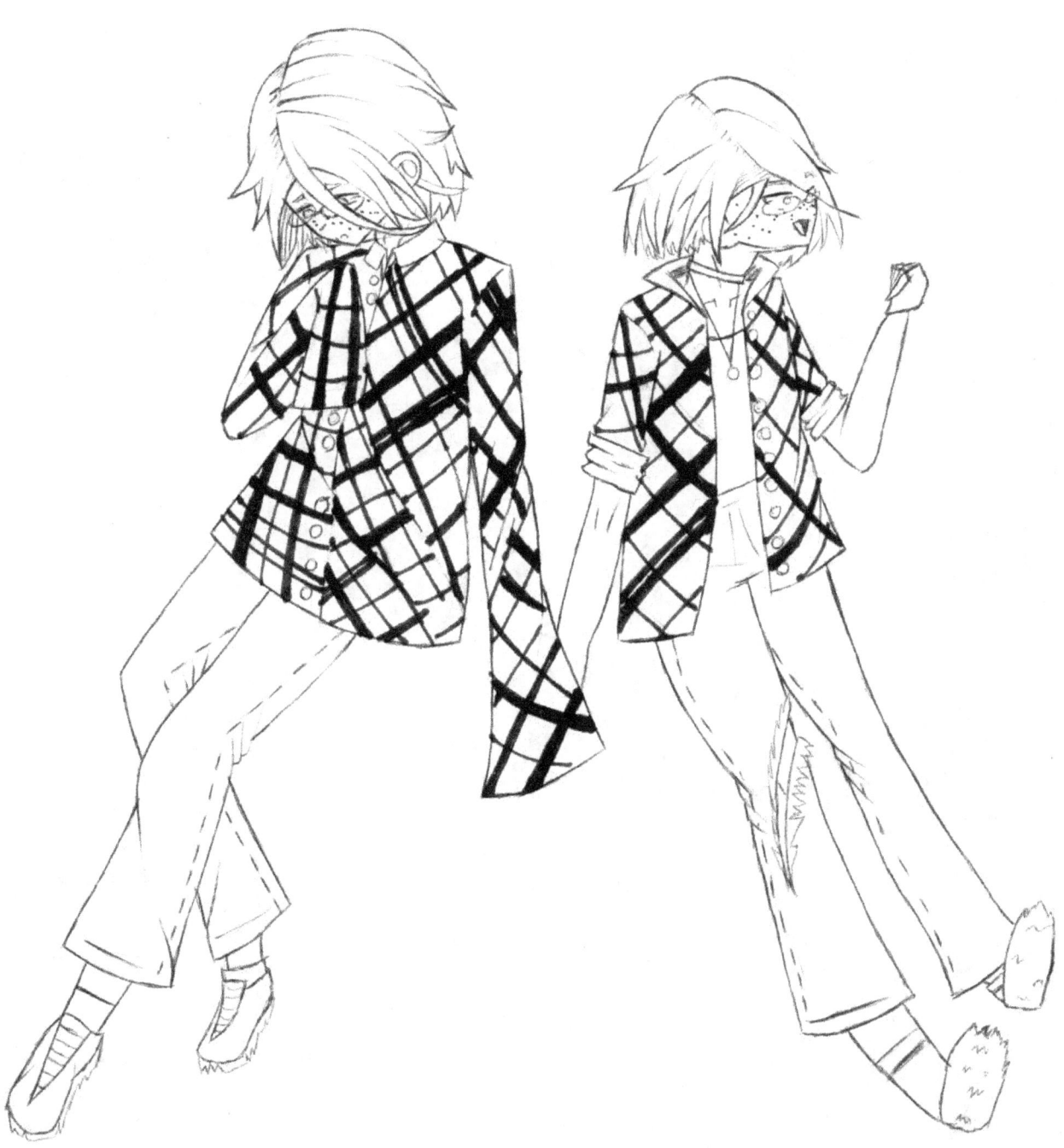

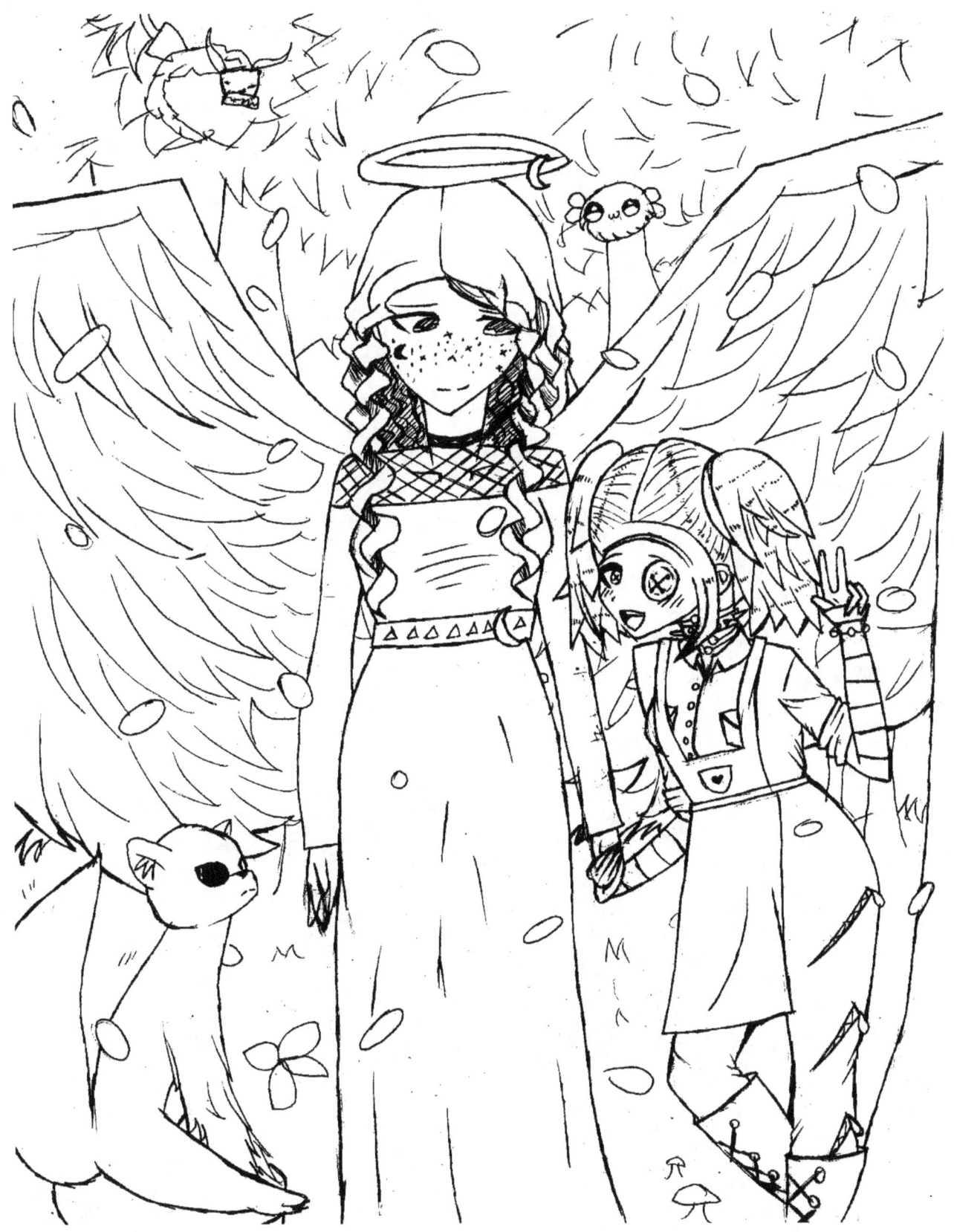

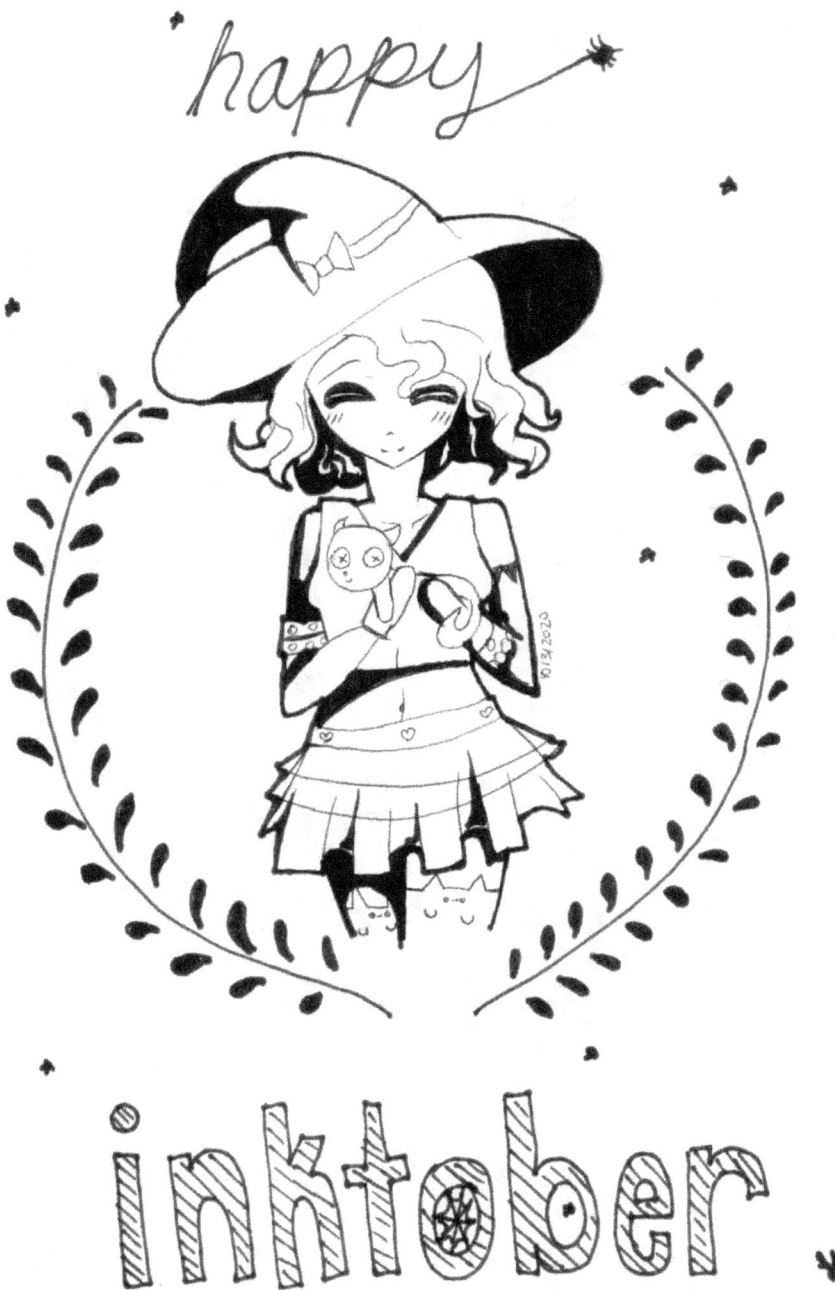

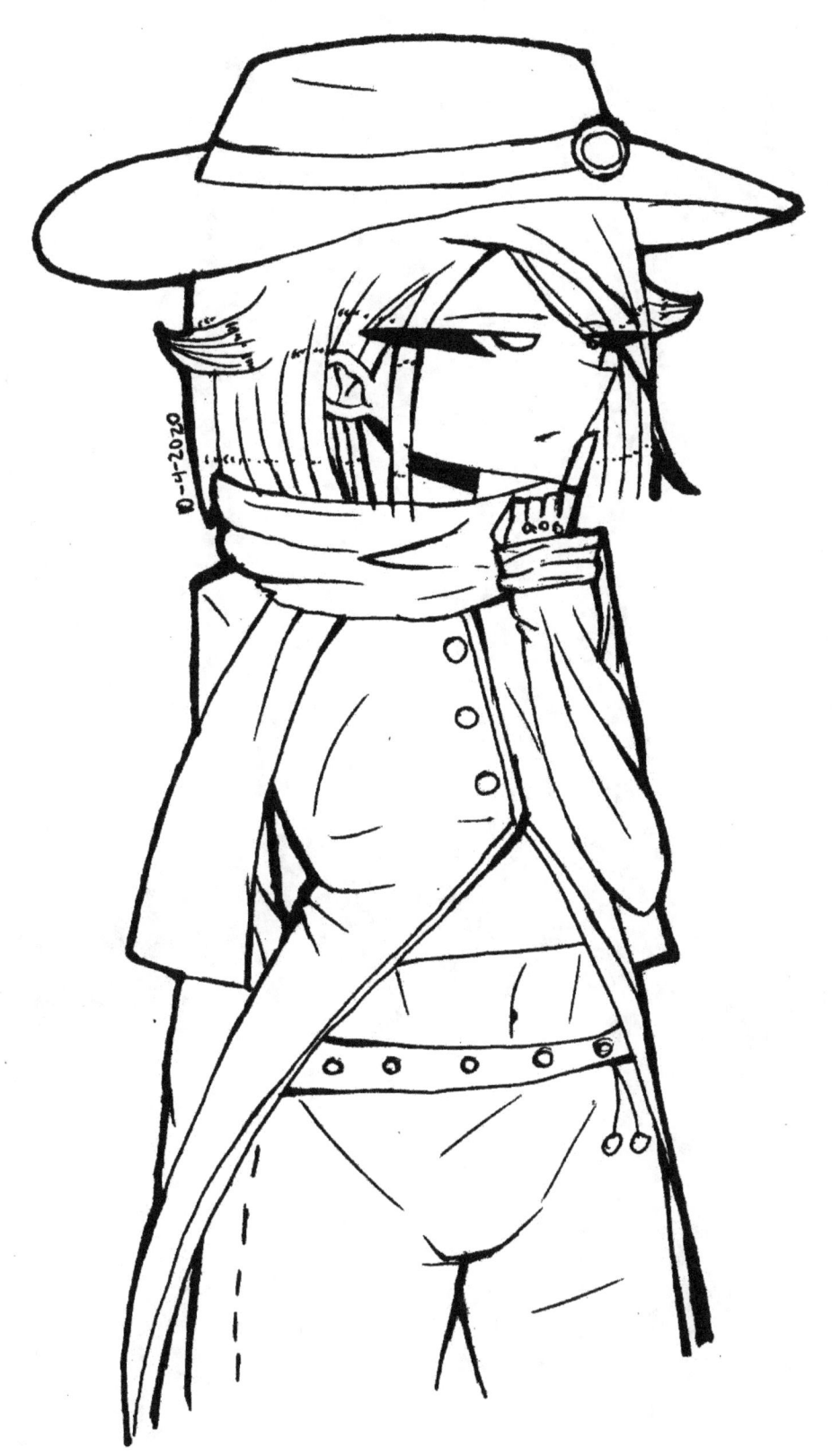

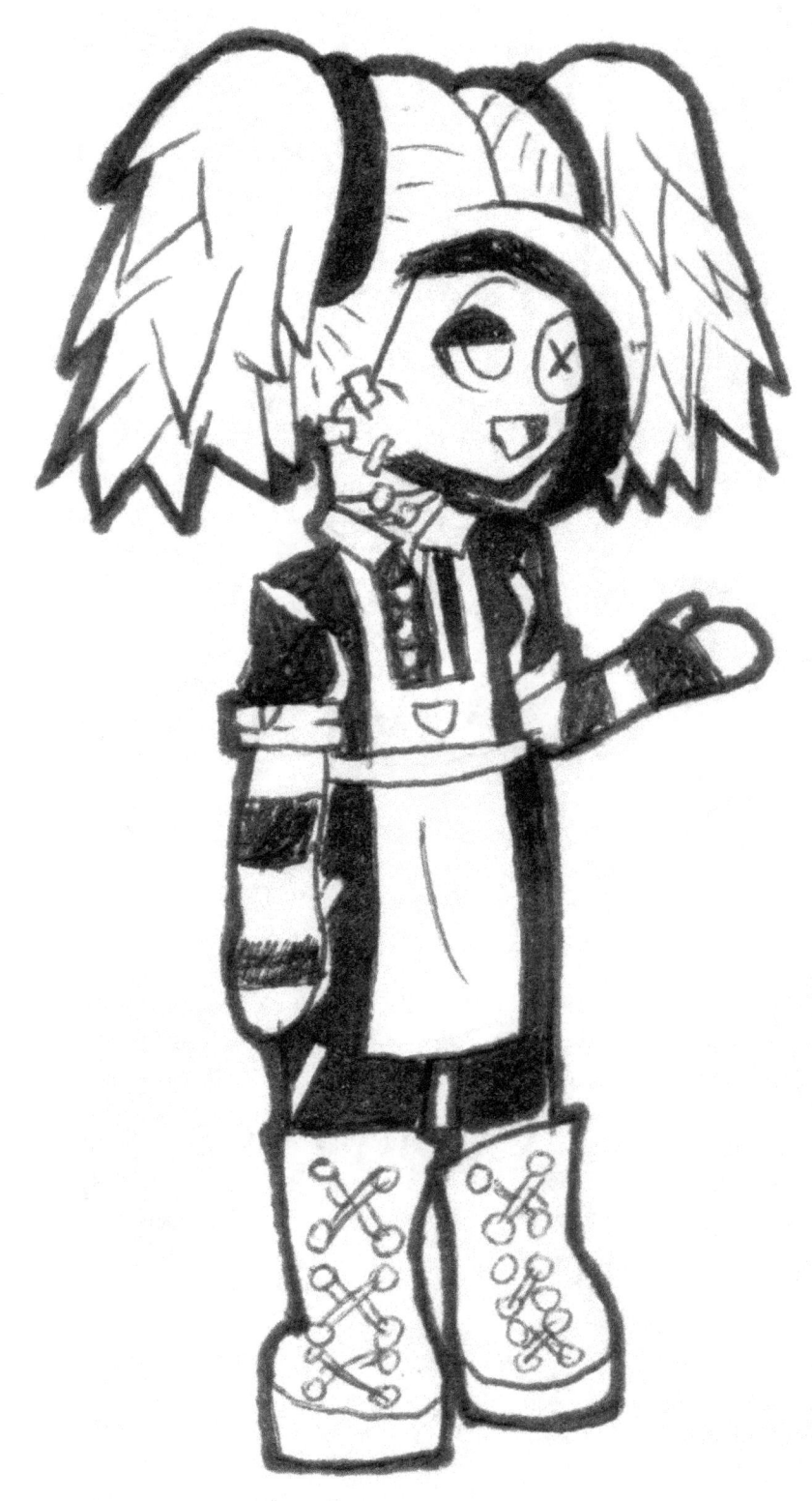

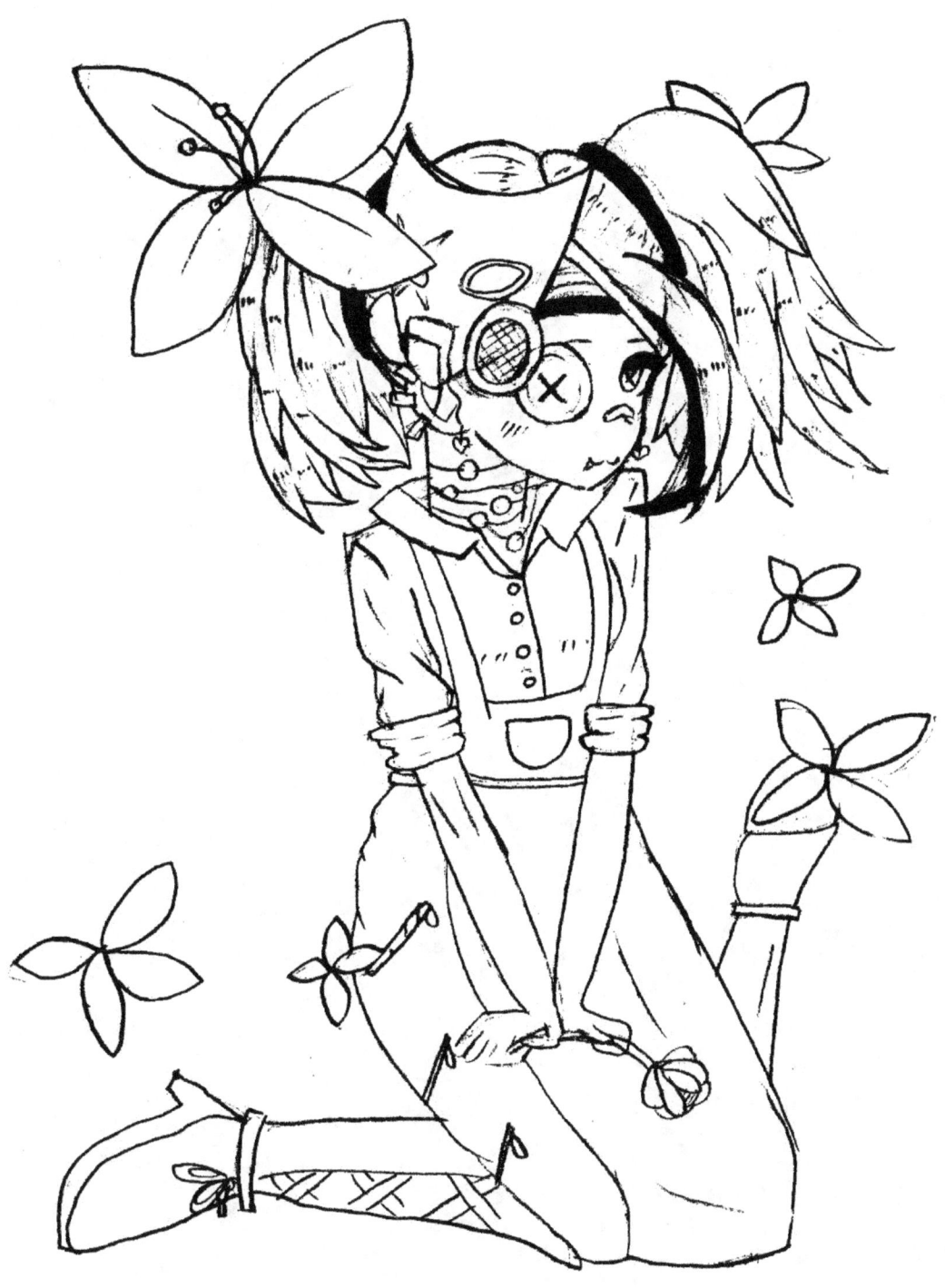

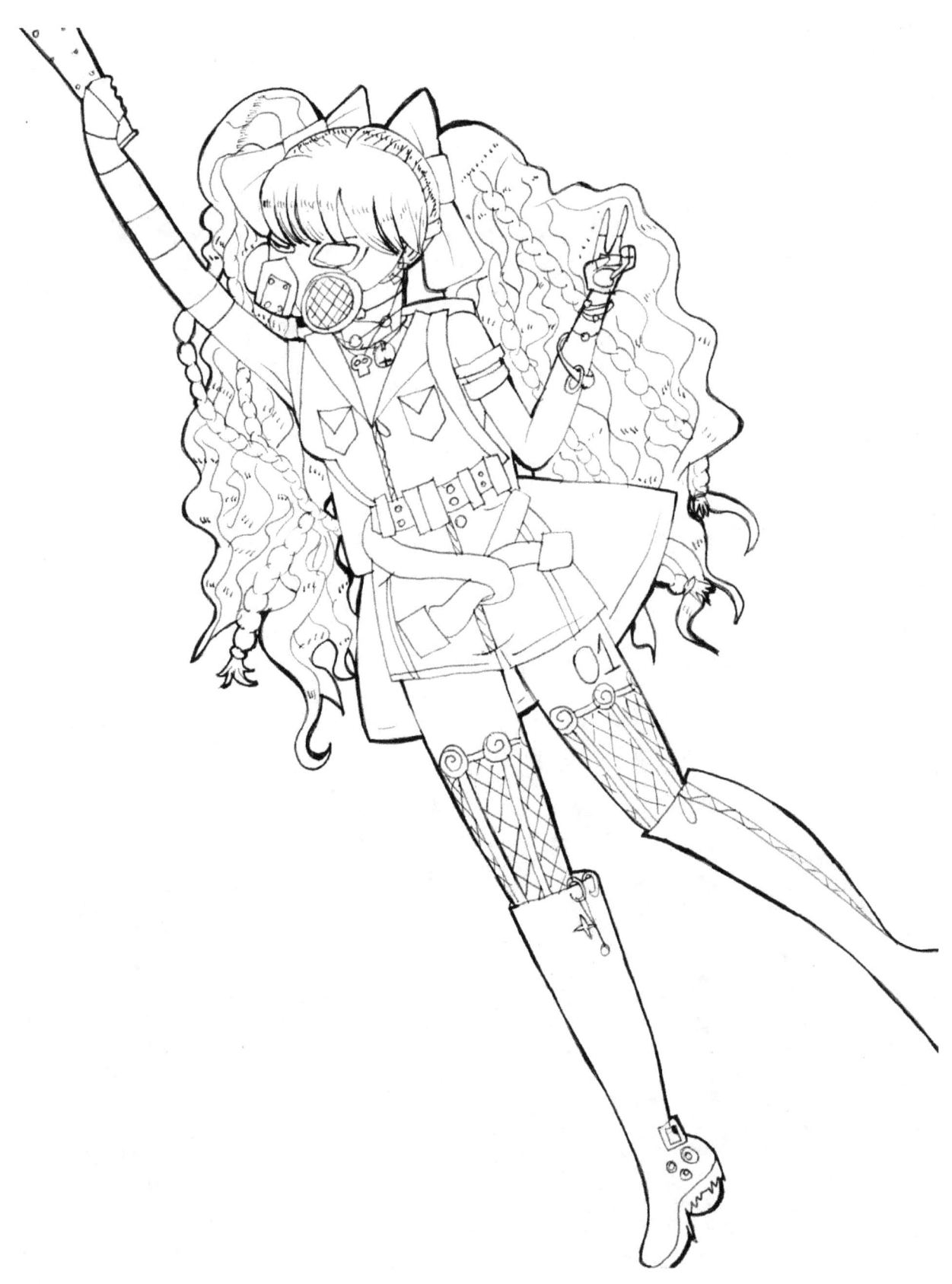

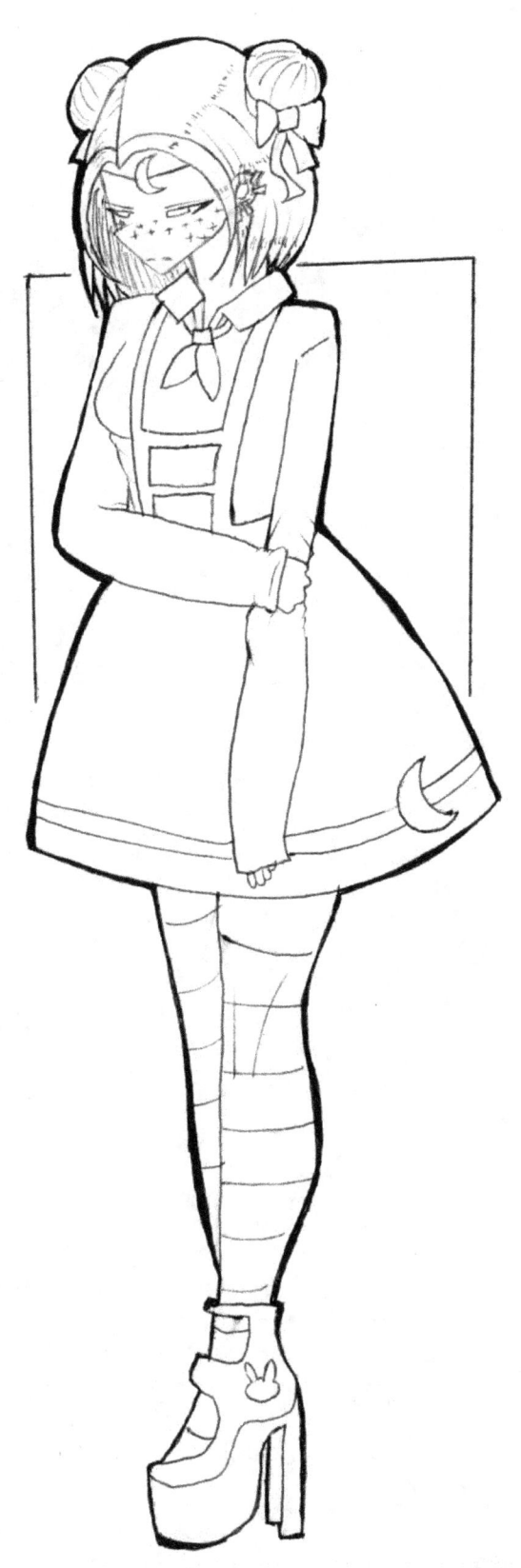

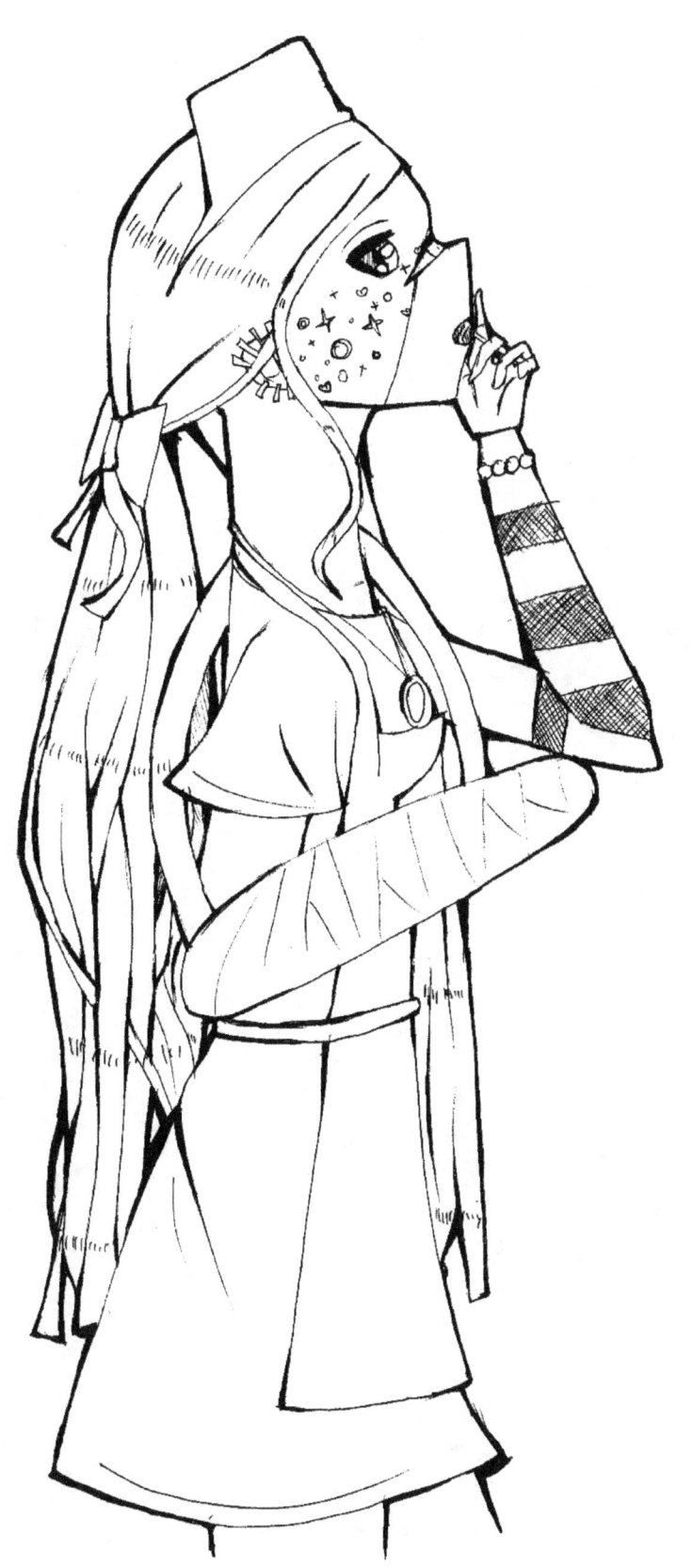

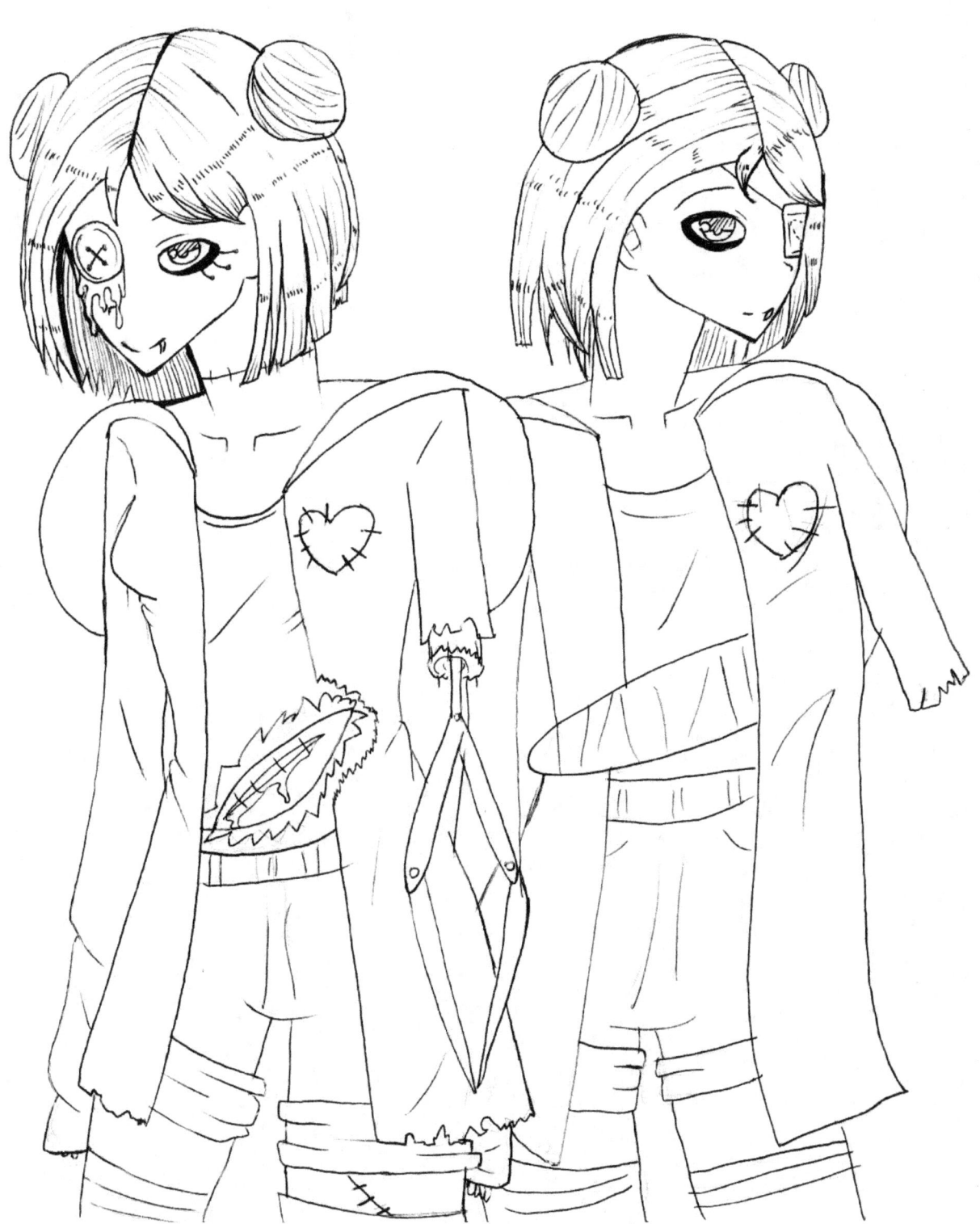

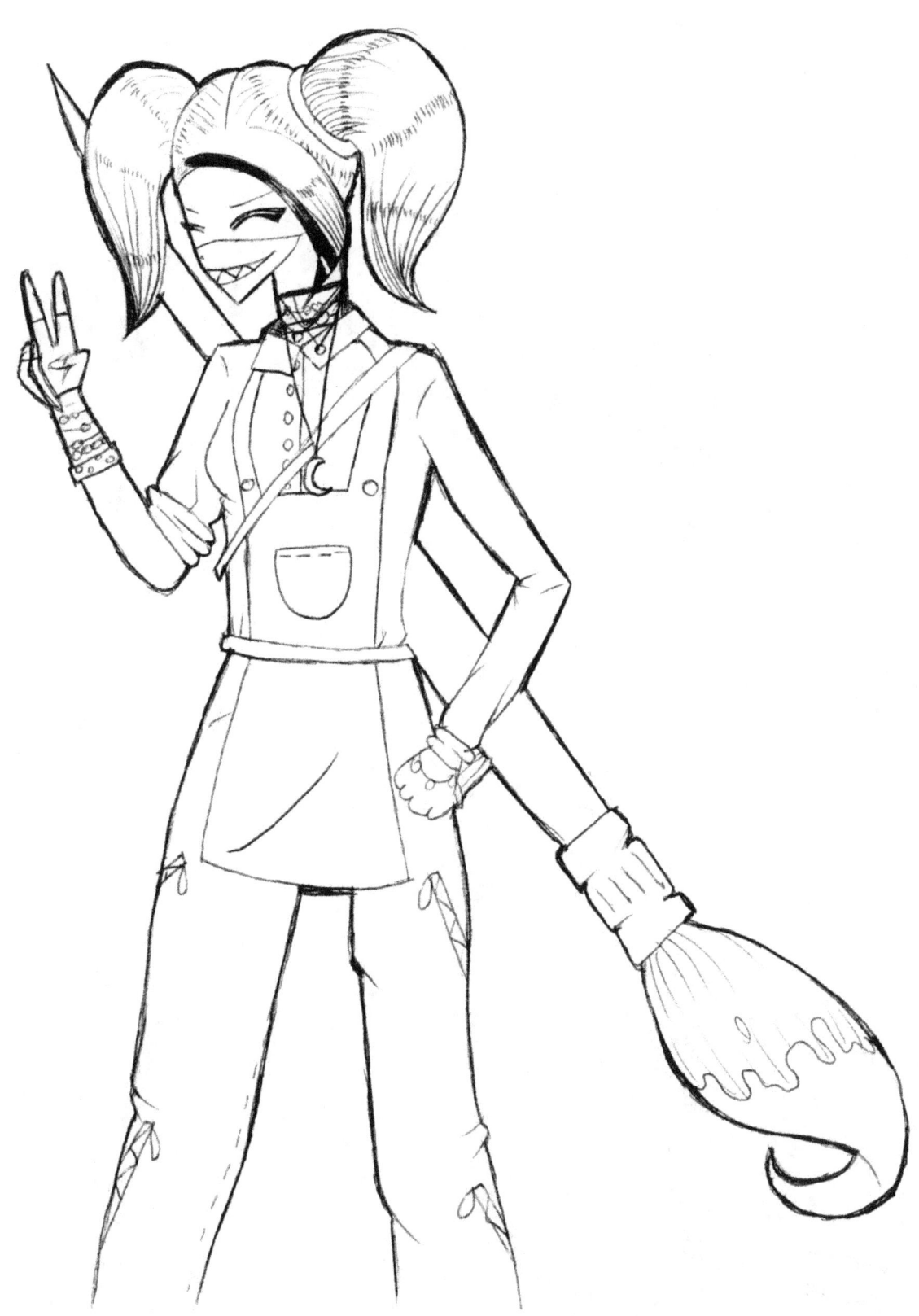

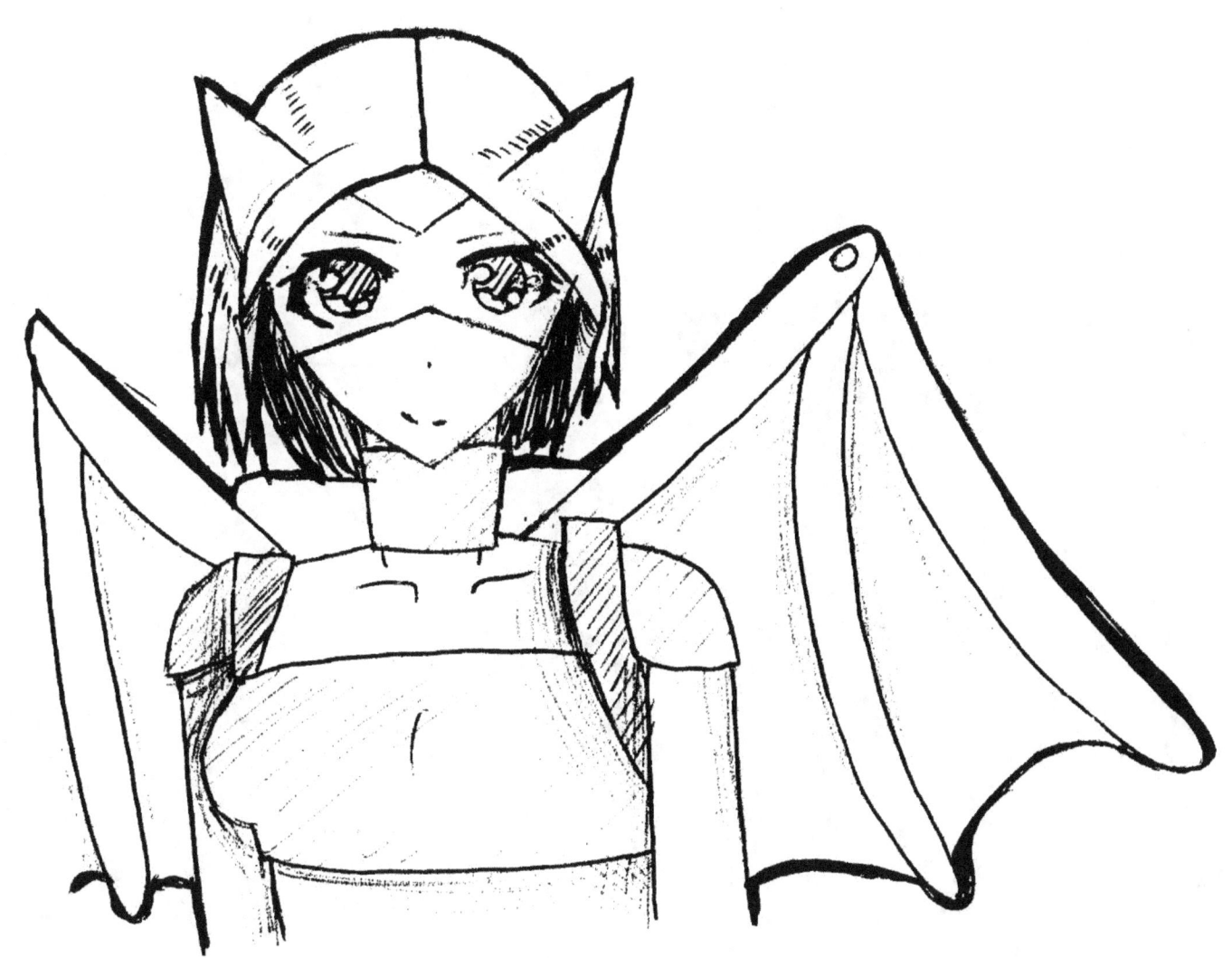

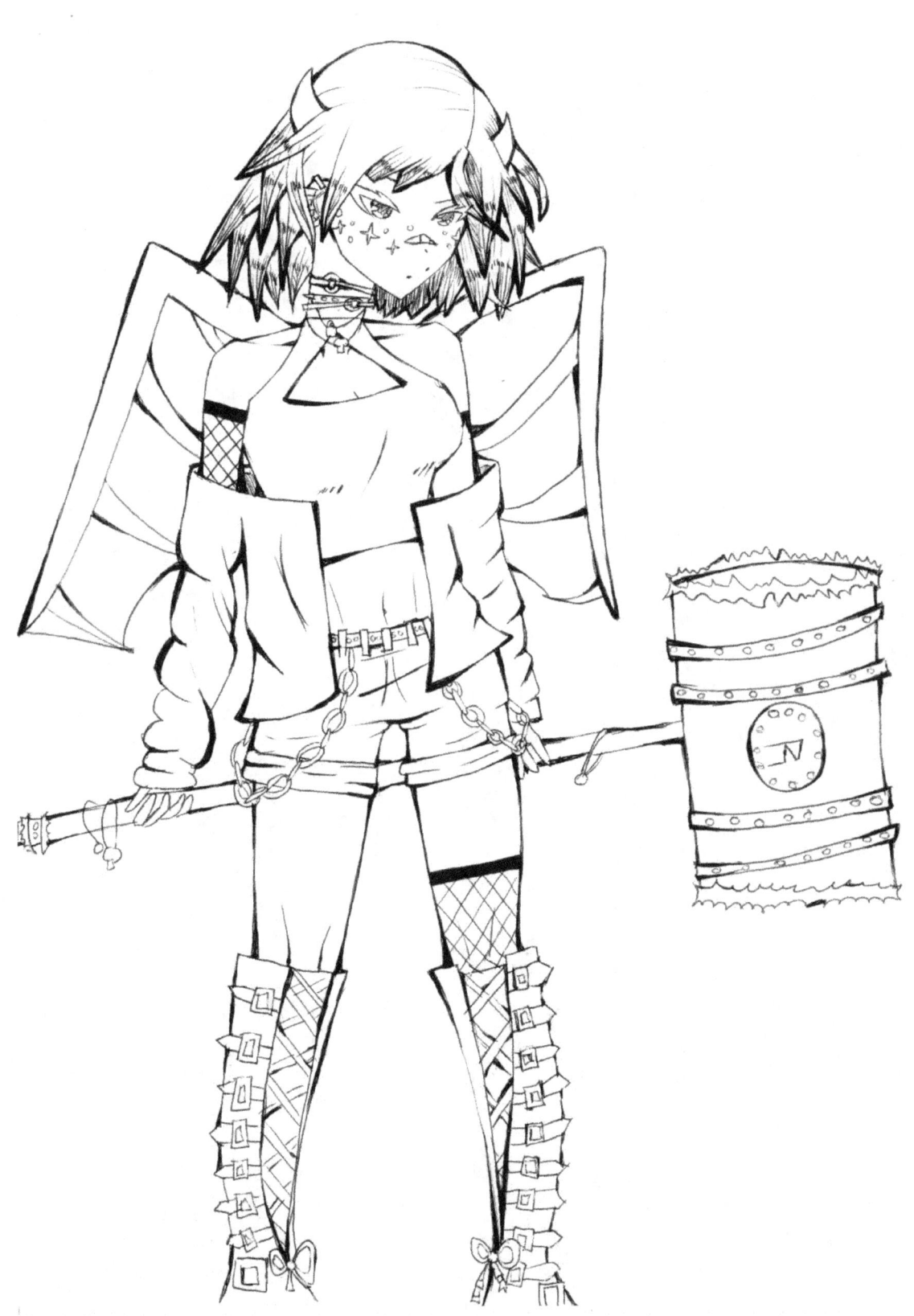

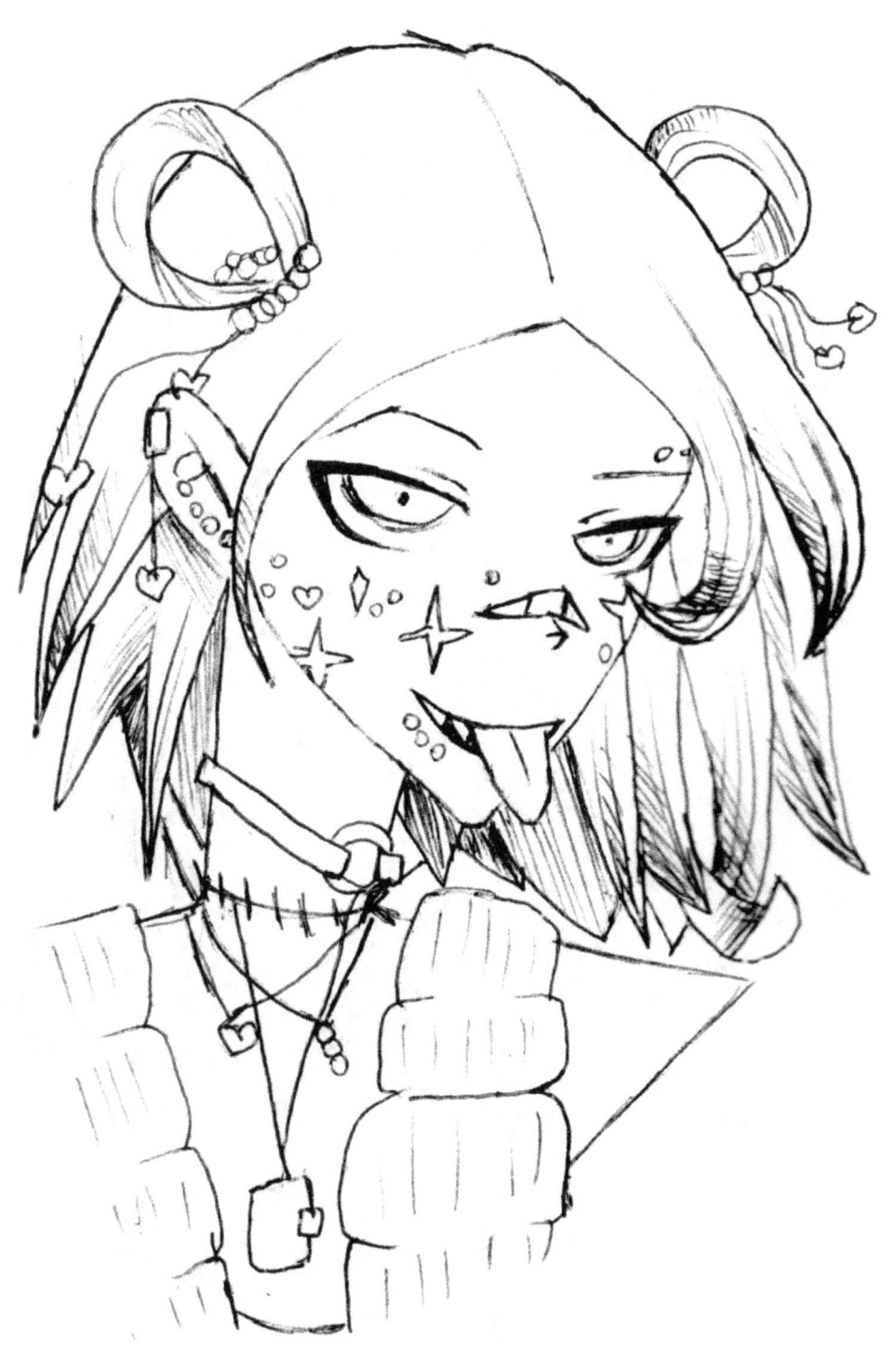

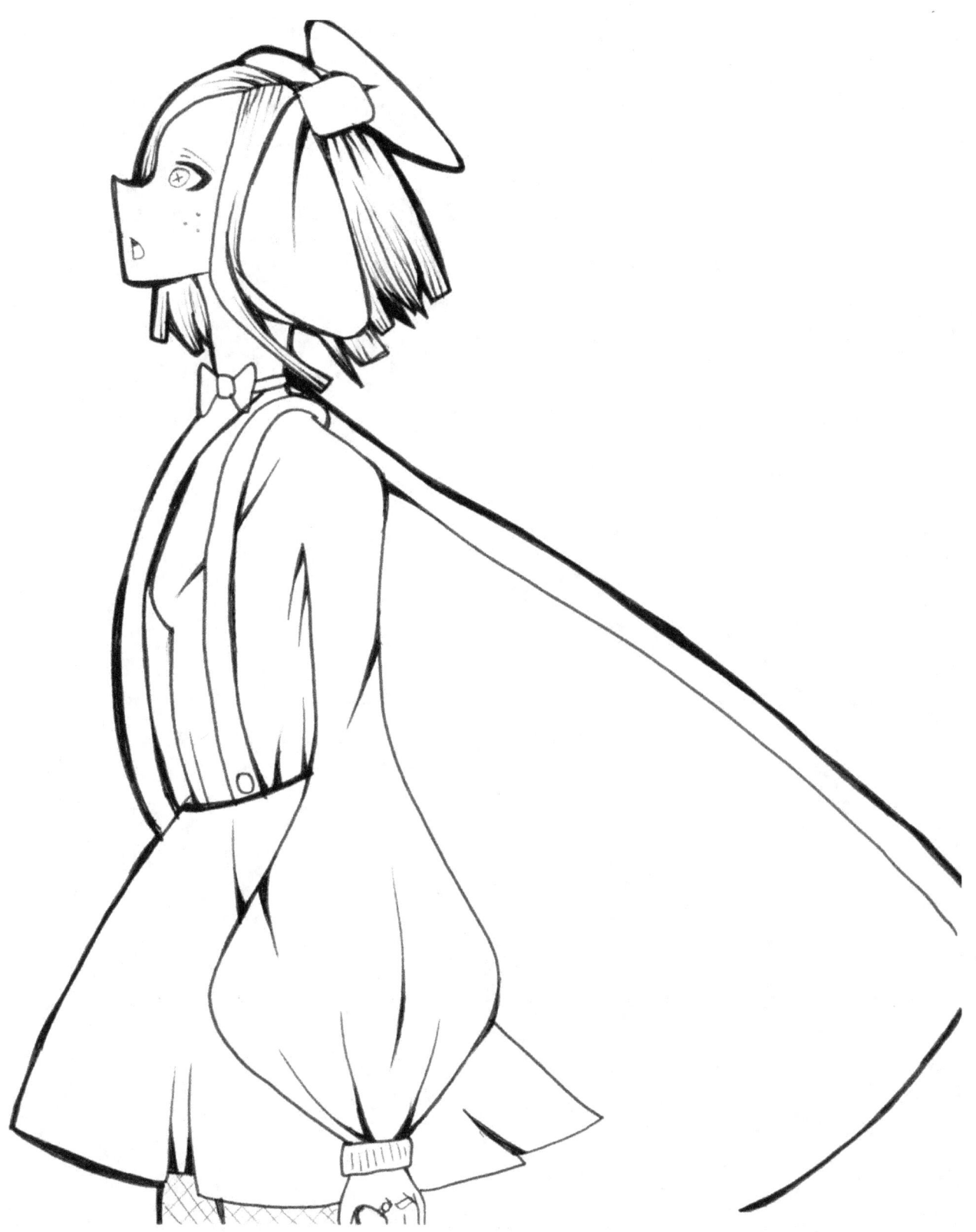

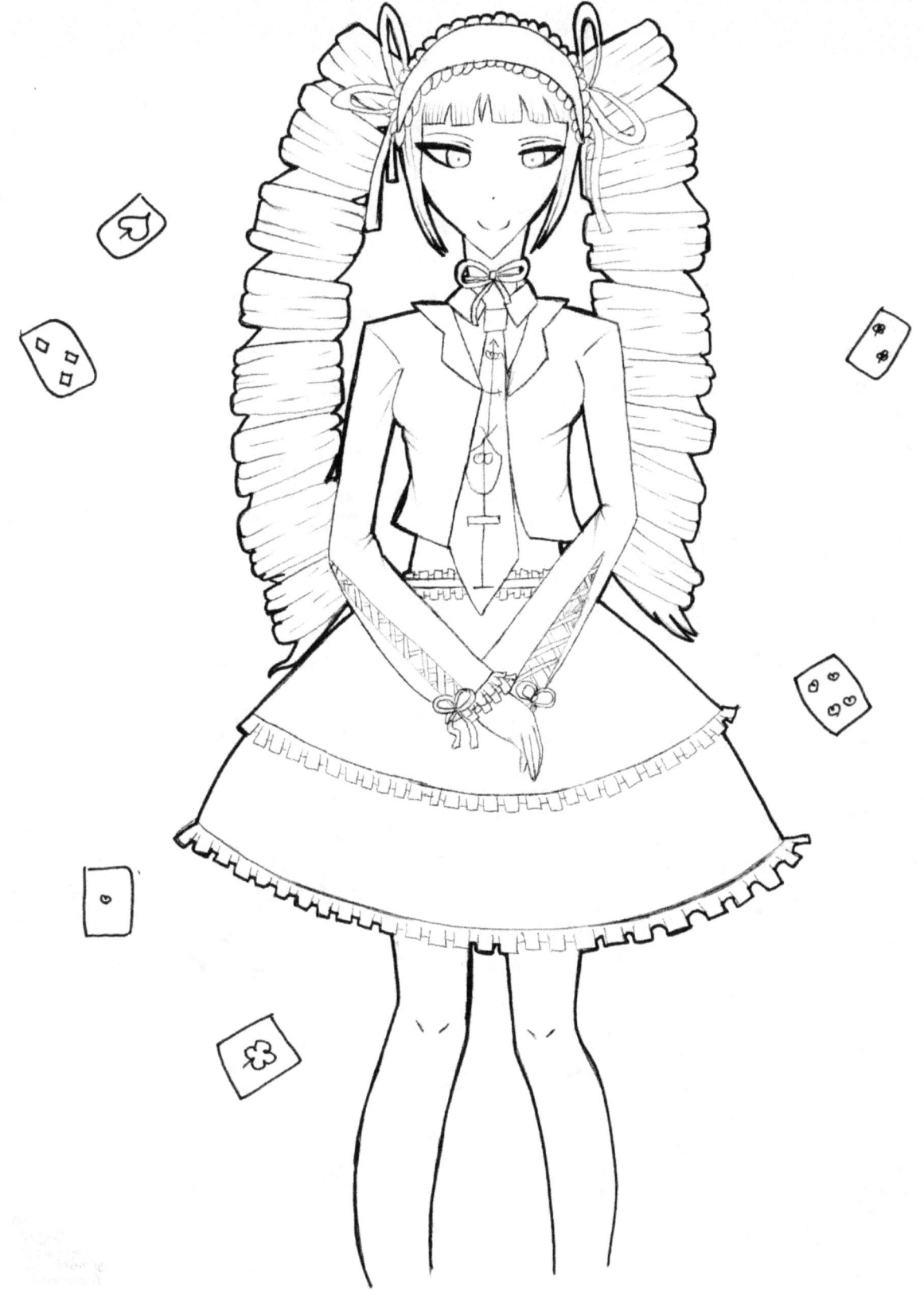

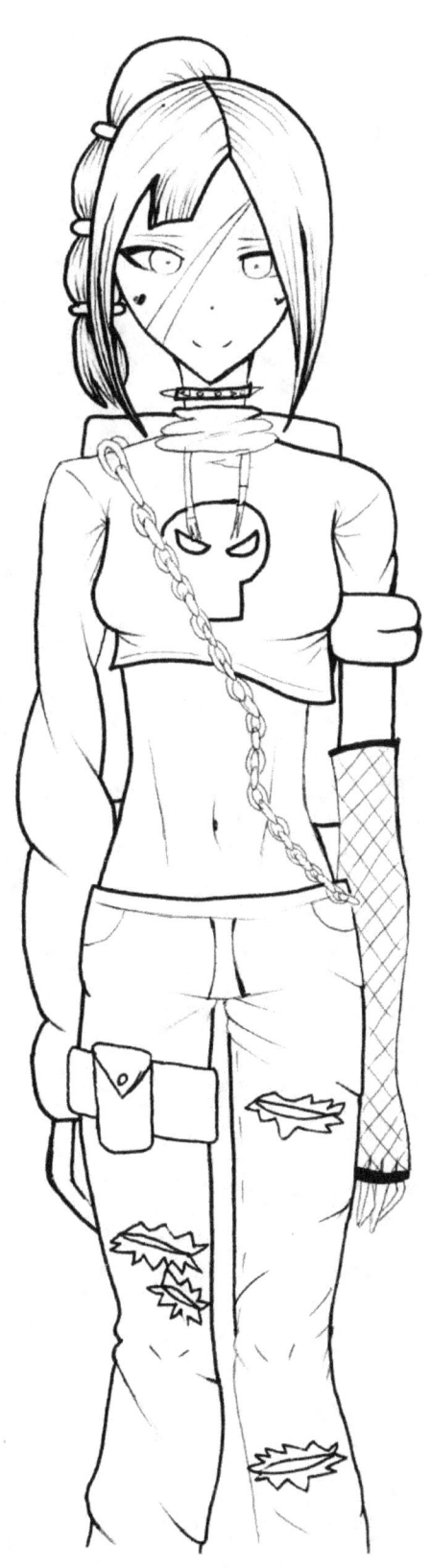

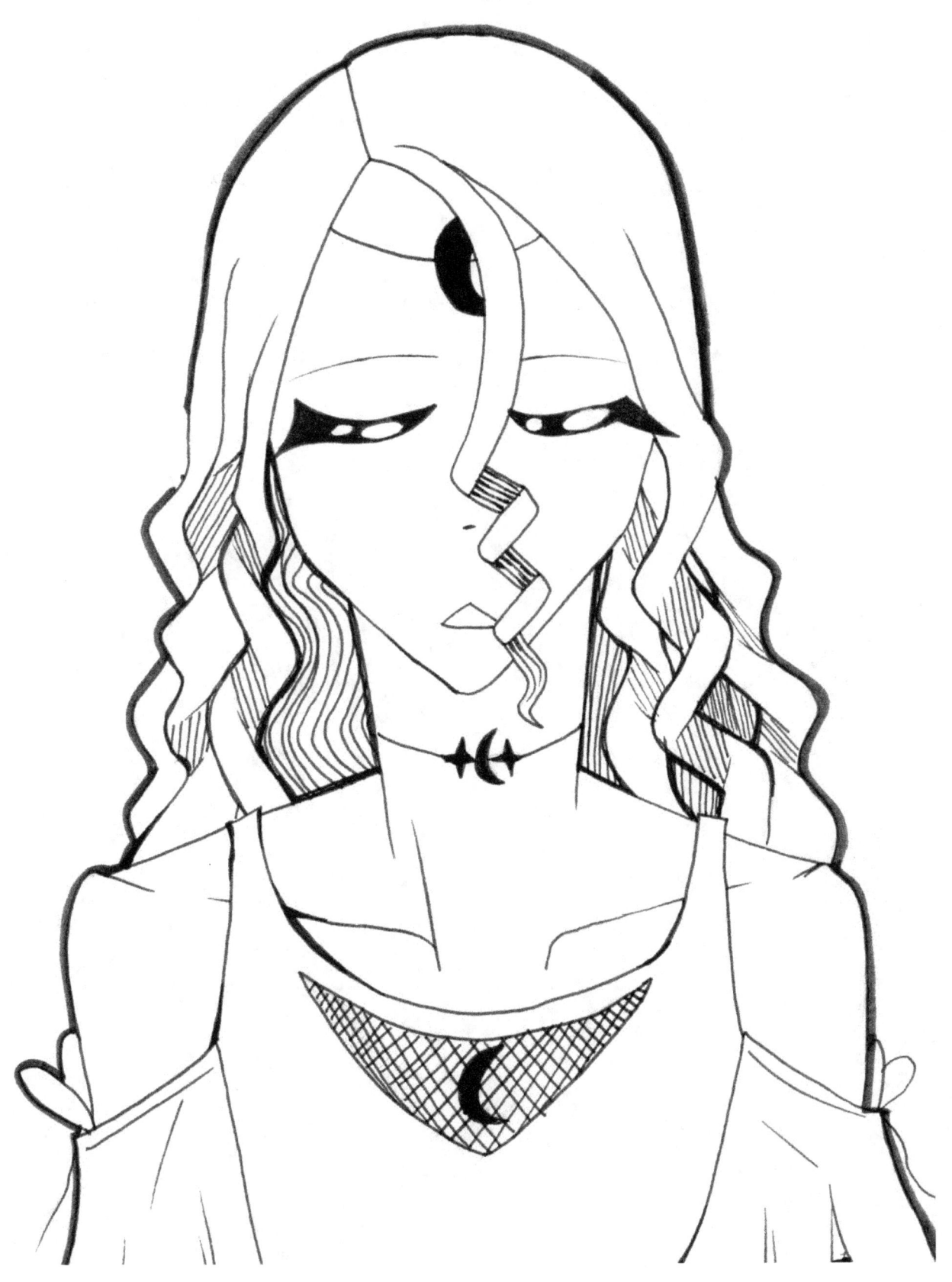

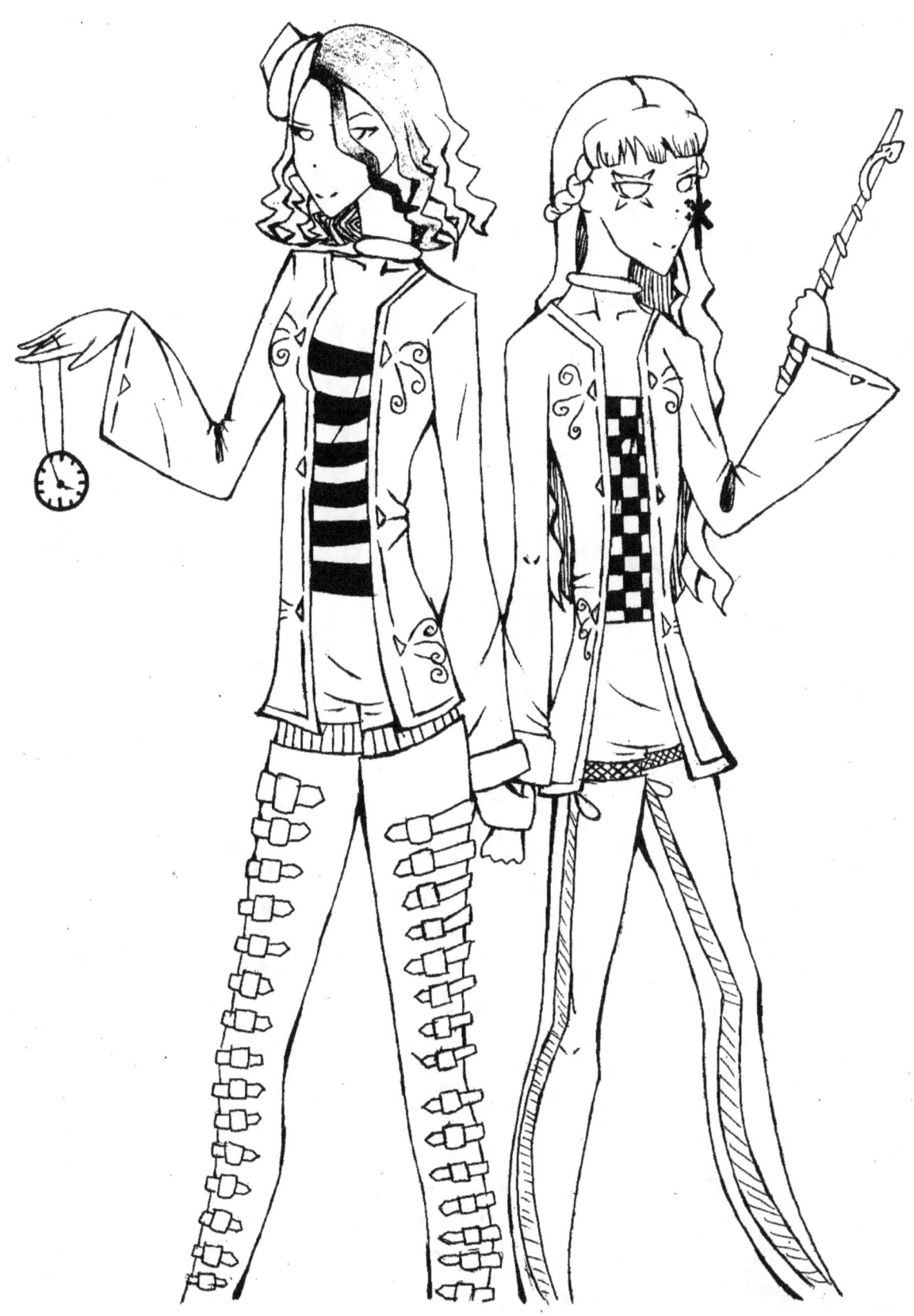

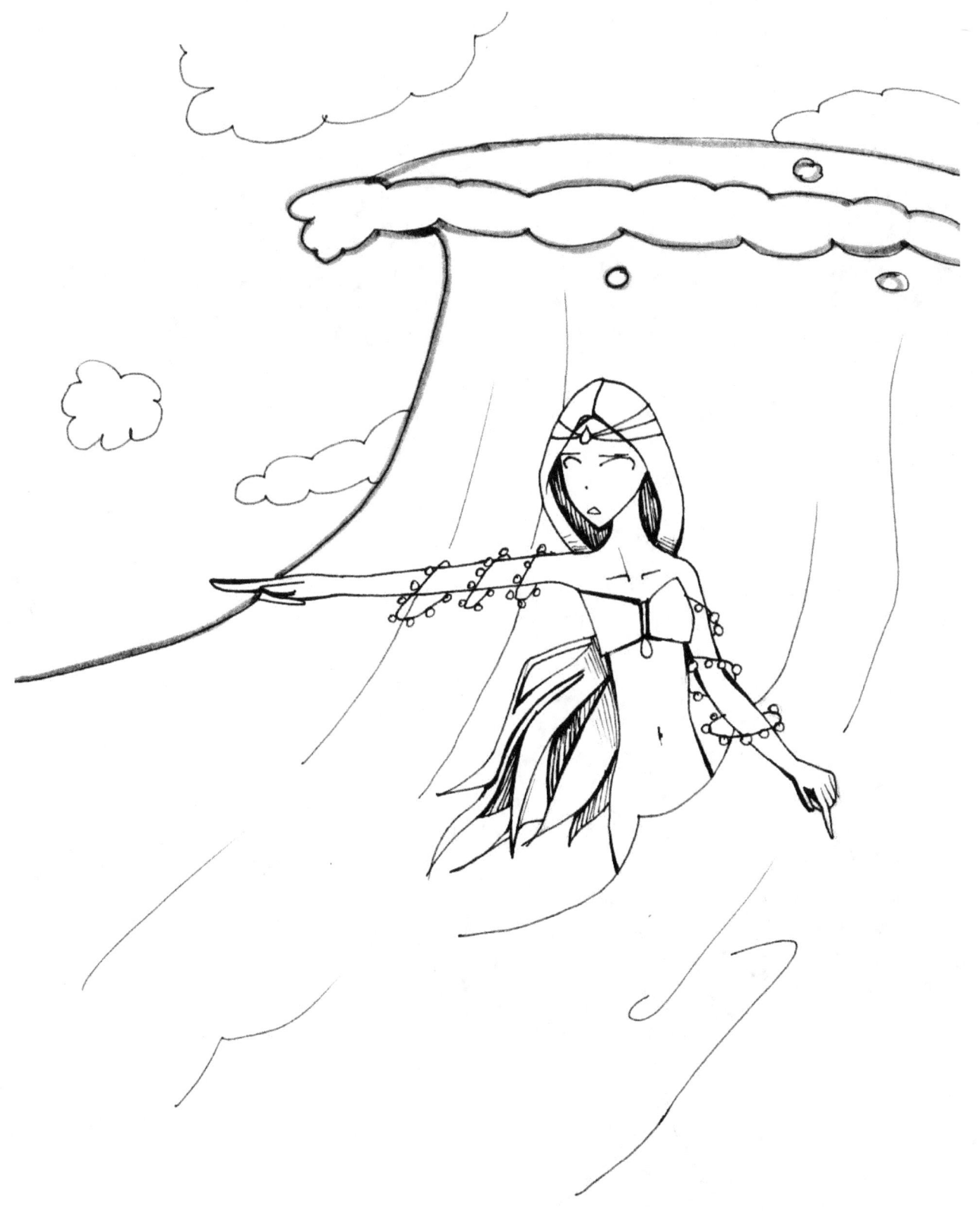

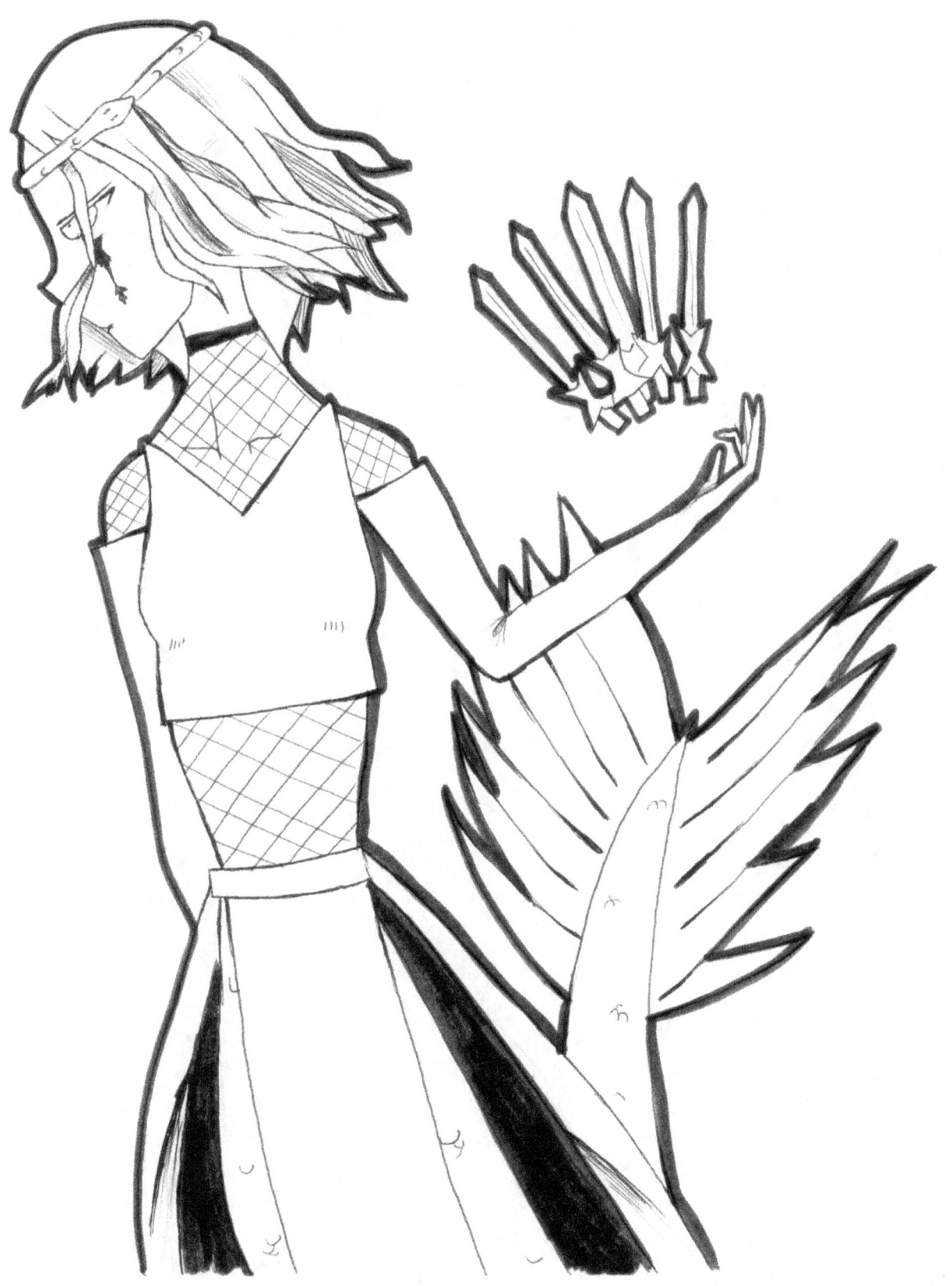

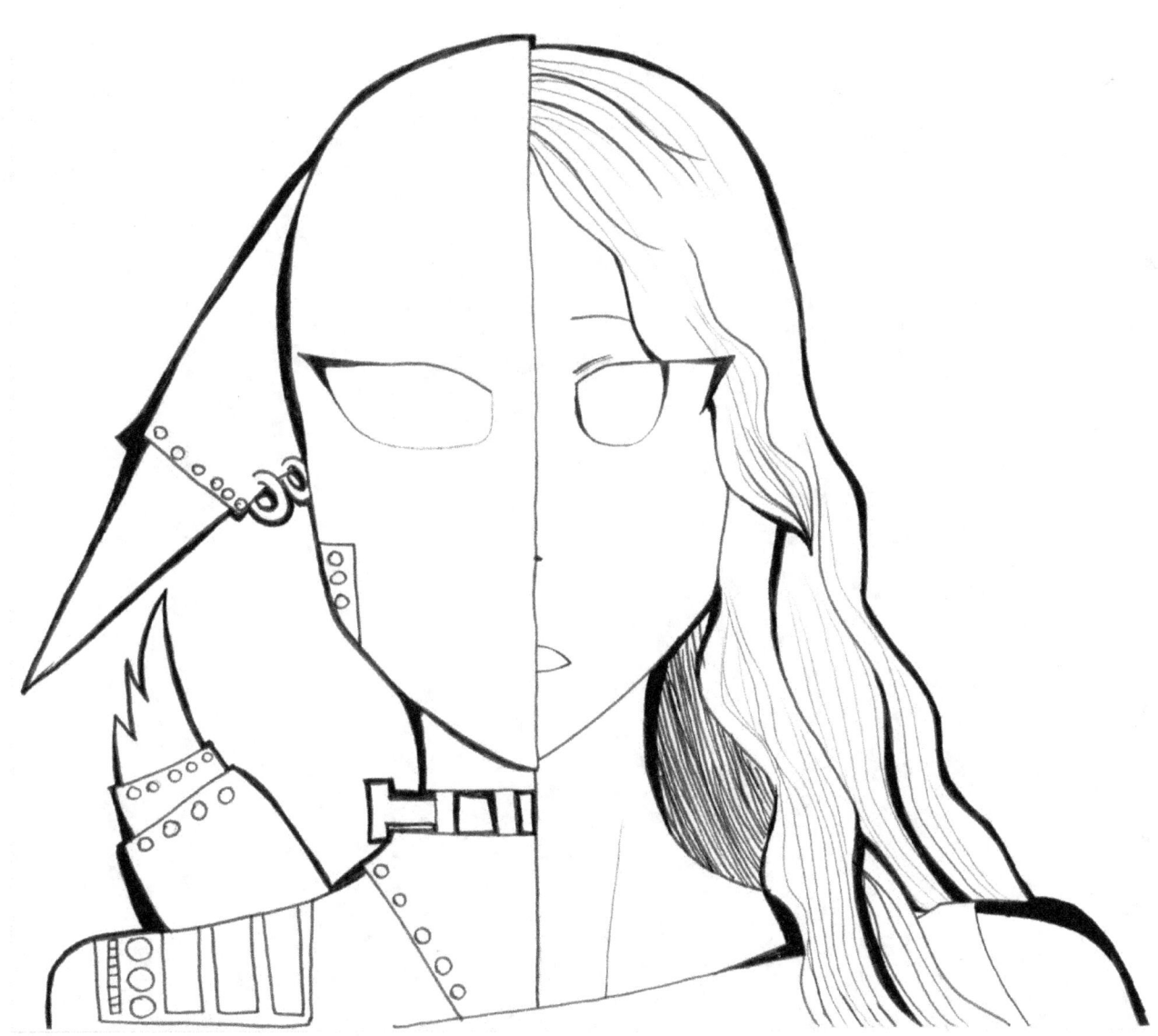

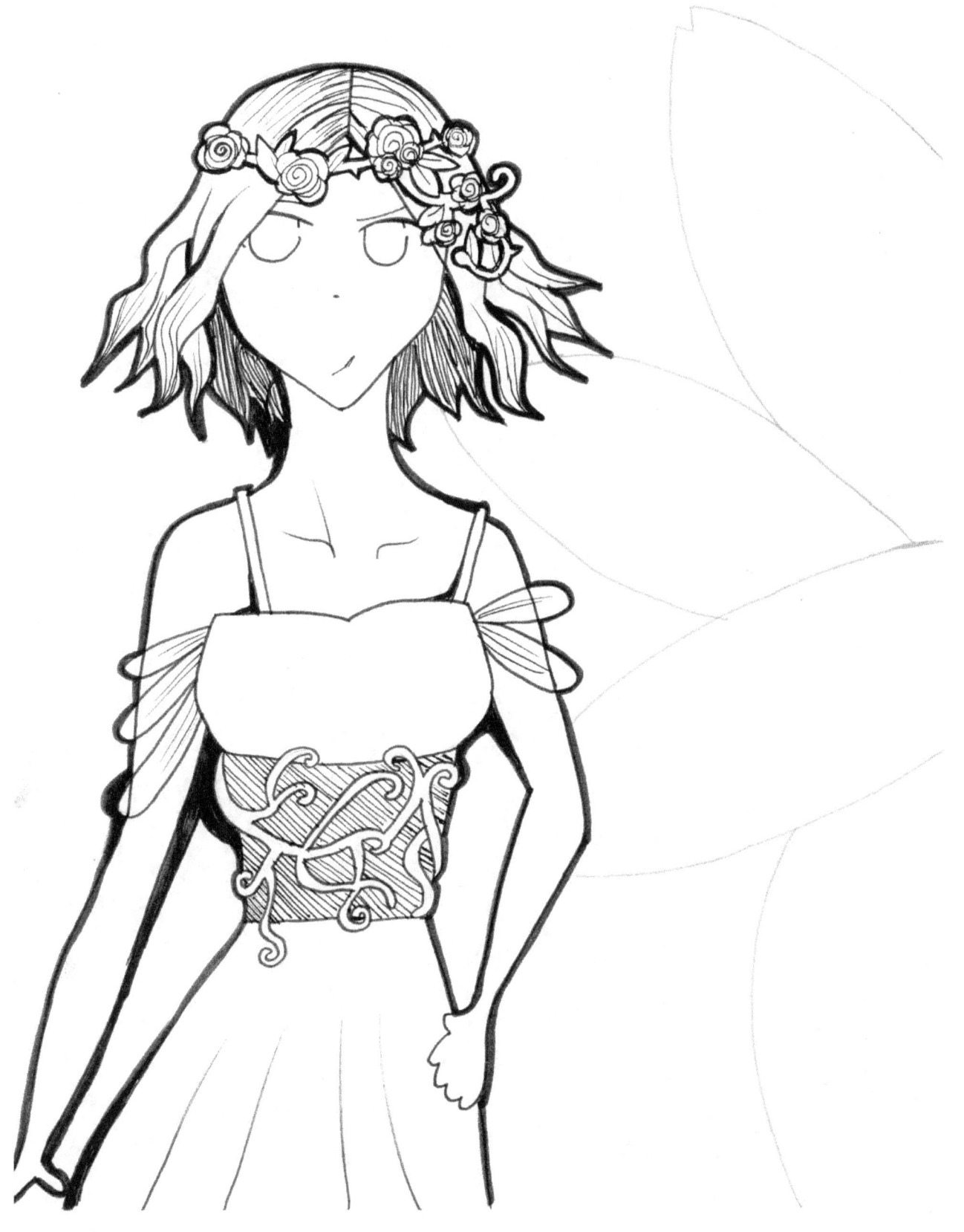

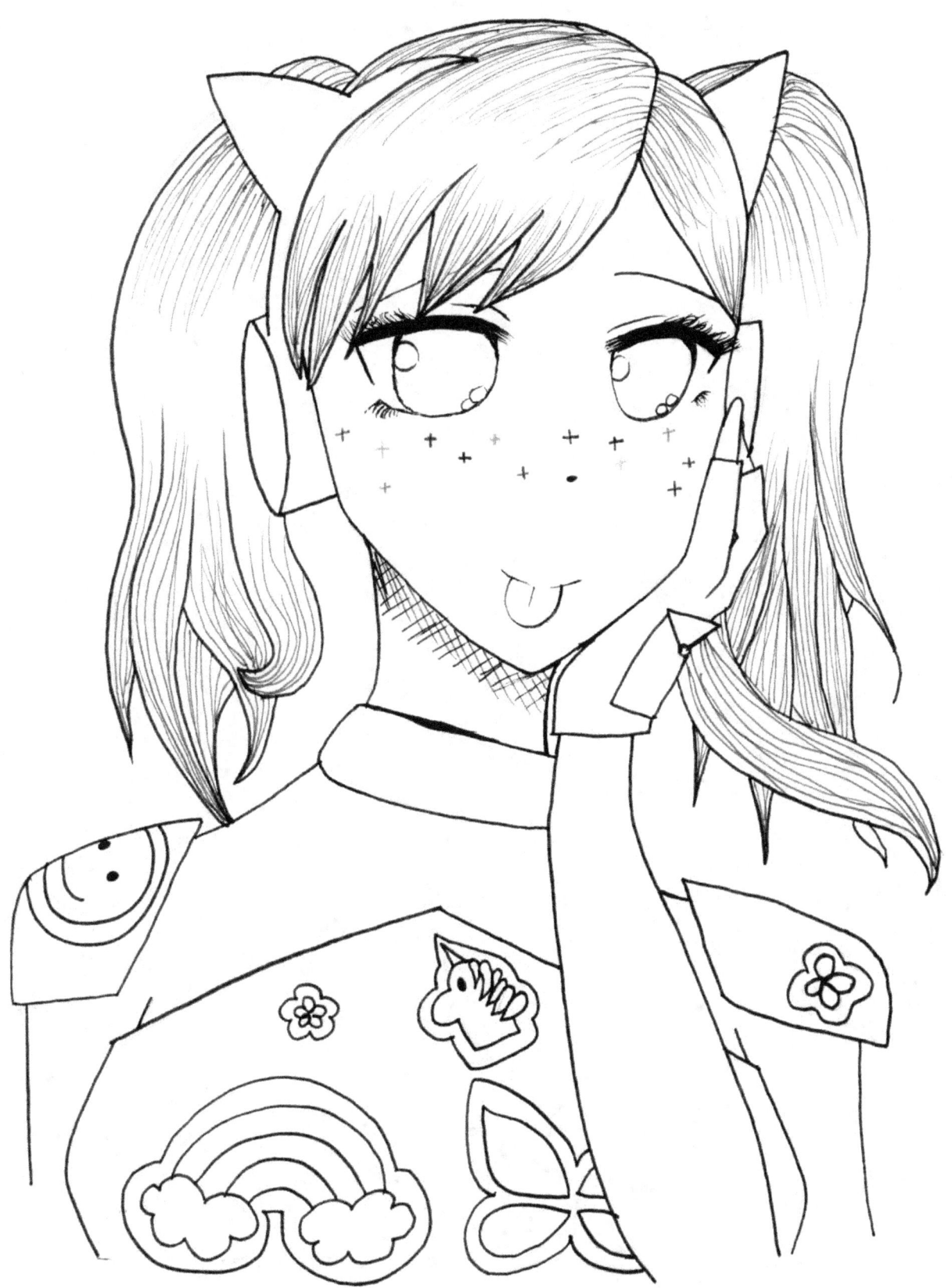

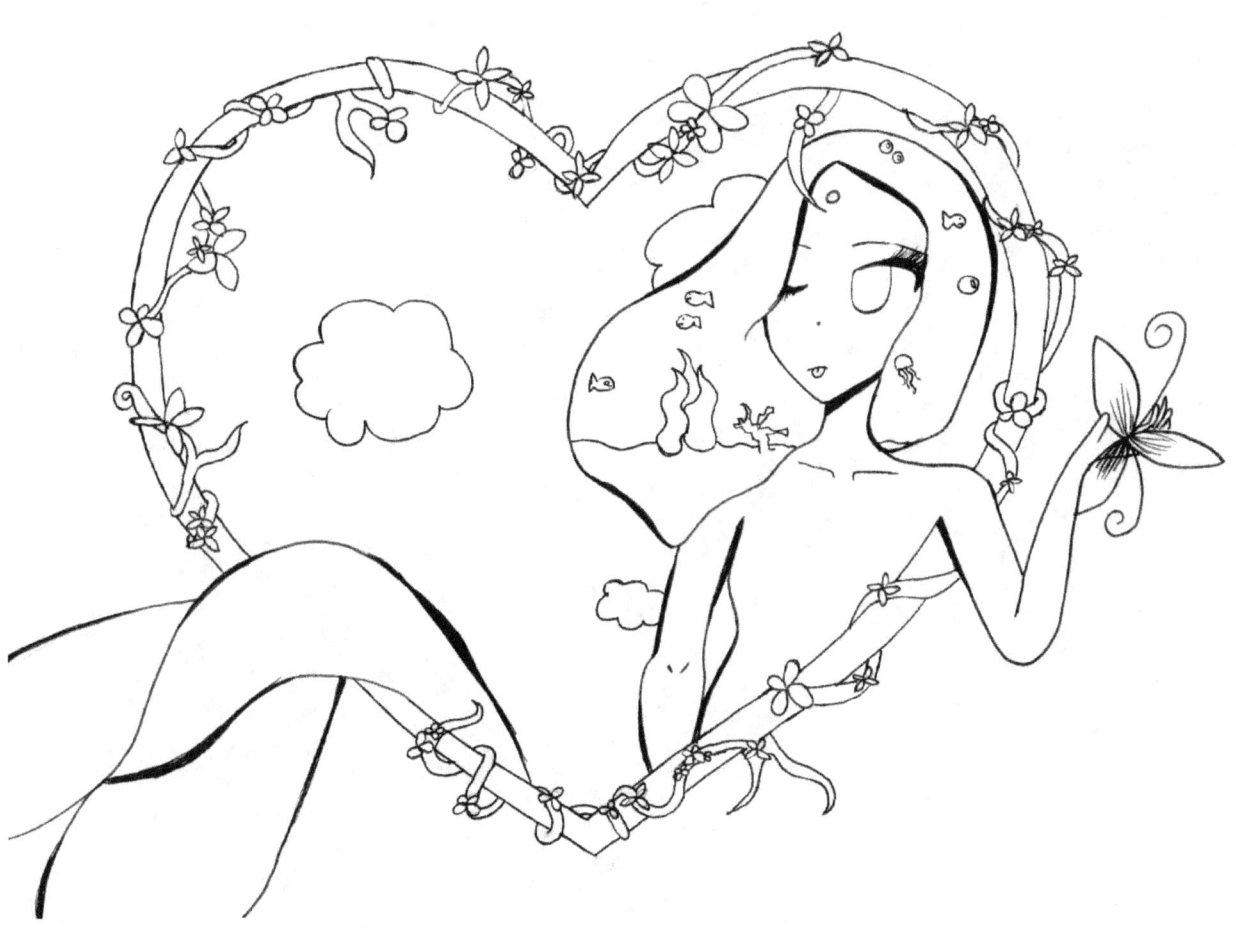

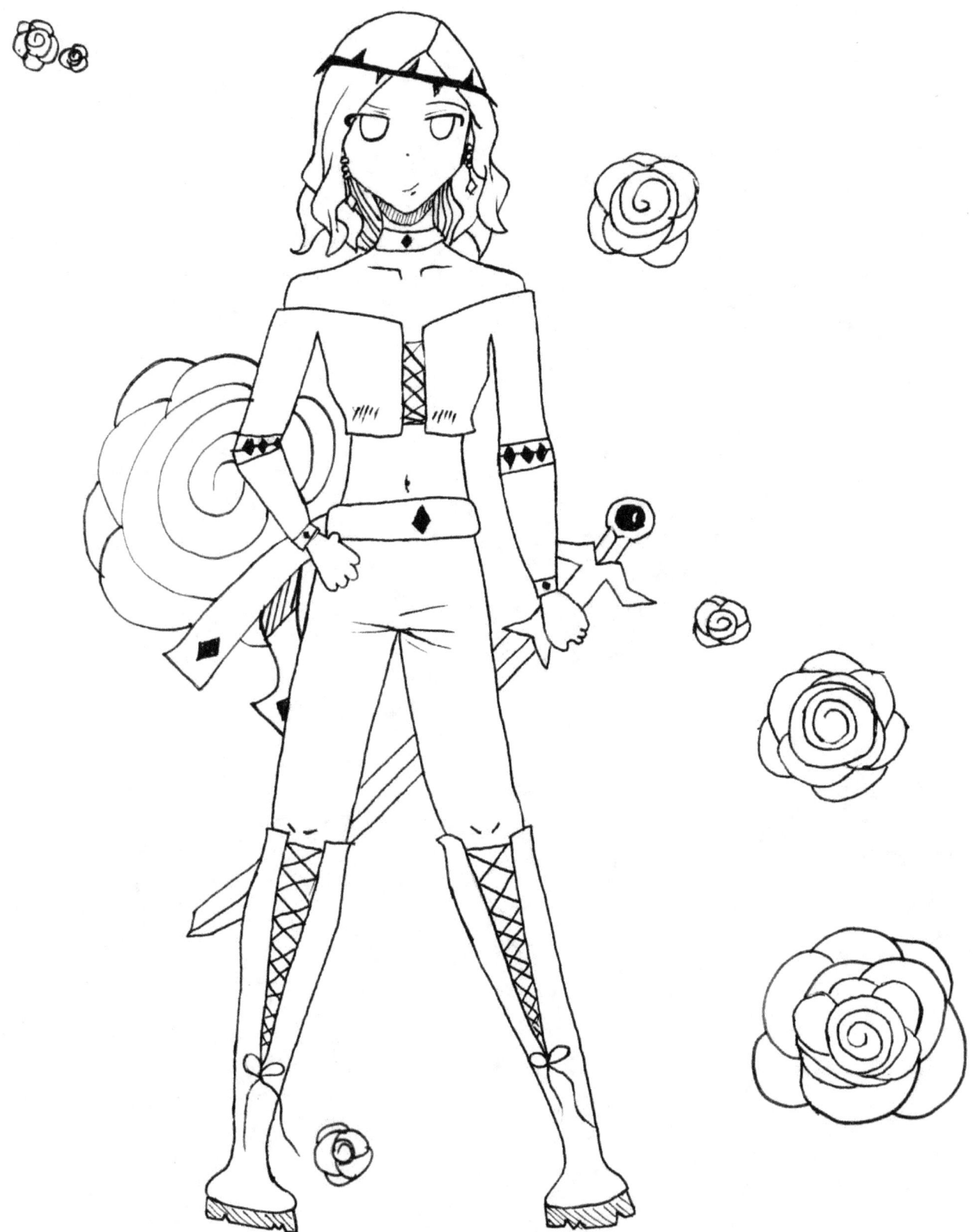

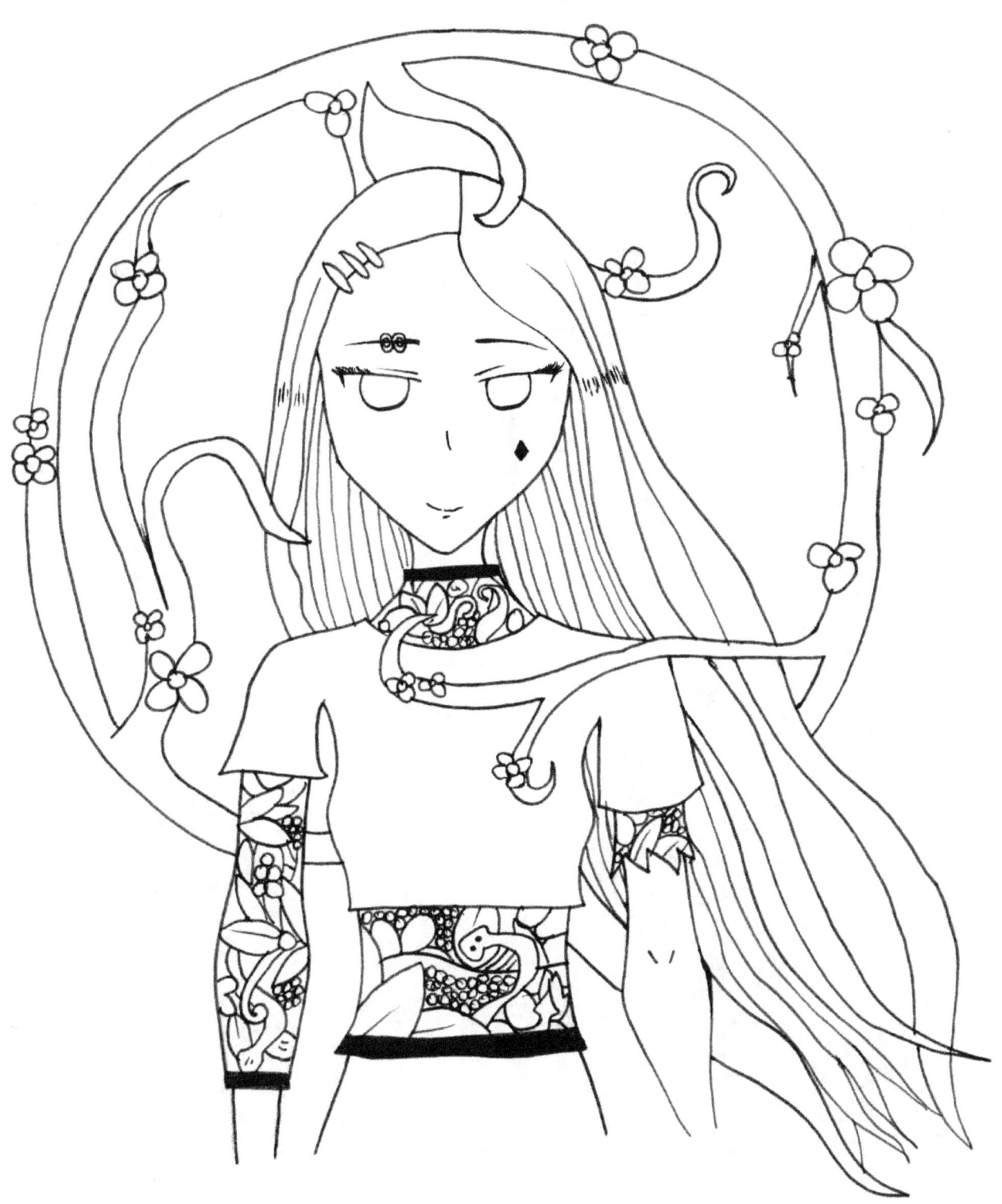

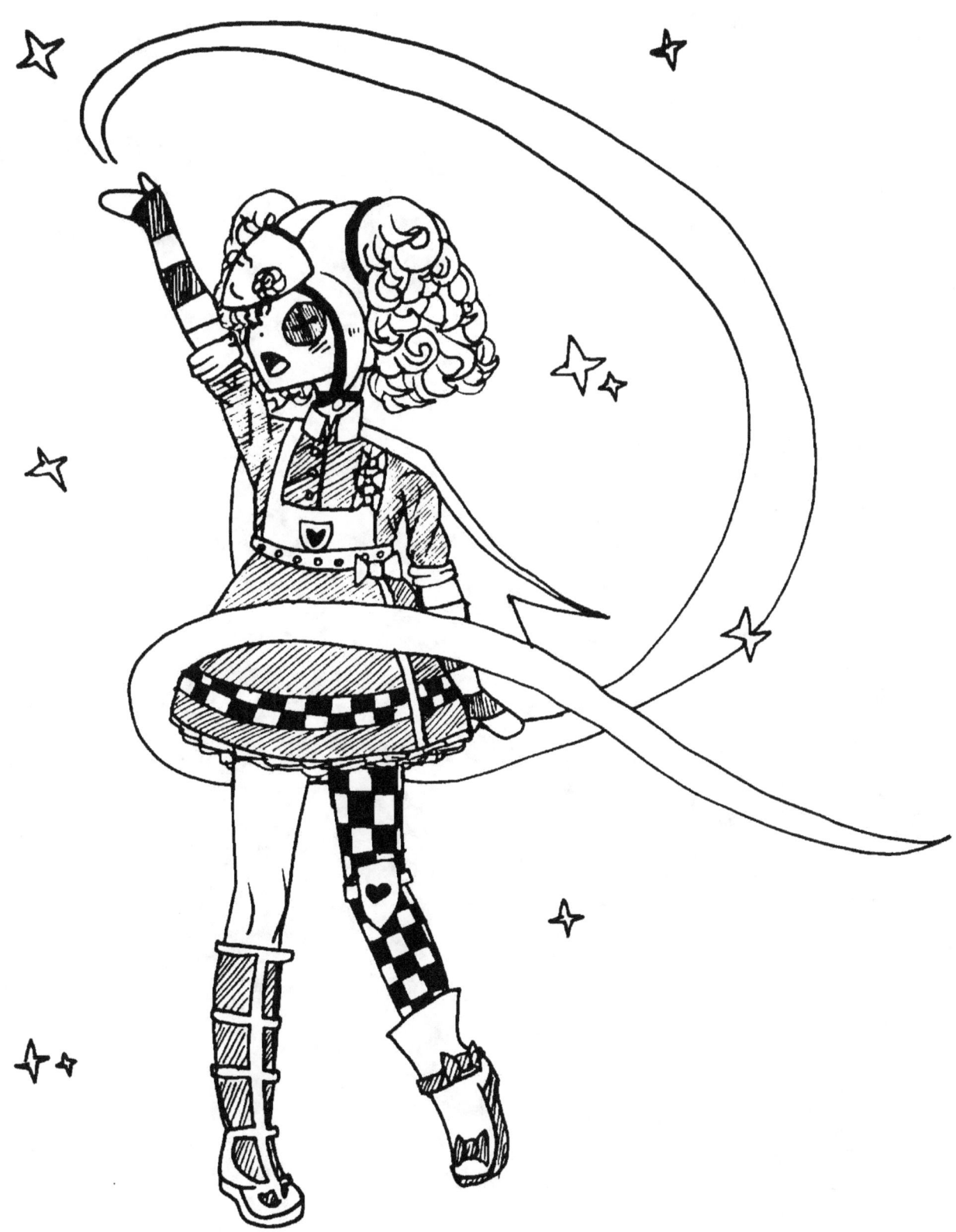

ABOUT THE AUTHOR

Jessica Metzger is a prolific artist and author. This is Jessica's second coloring book. Although each picture requires 1-3 hours to draw, Jessica created them because they were fun, and she hopes you have as much fun coloring them as she had making them. She is currently a full-time student, yet she still finds time to work on more art projects and novels, and she hopes you get to see them in the future.

Novels by Jessica Metzger:

    A Crack in the World
    A Glitch in the World

Coloring books by Jessica Metzger:

    Anime Coloring Book
    Anime Coloring Book: Volume 2

www.ingramcontent.com/pod-product-compliance
Lightning Source LLC
Chambersburg PA
CBHW080506220526
45465CB00006B/2391